I0412727

A growing list of your author's books
are attached in the back of this book
for your inspection.

Understanding Preventing and Eliminating Cancer

Features Natural Methods For Practical
and Effective Use

Lloyd E. McIlveen

Order this book online at www.trafford.com
or email orders@trafford.com

Most Trafford titles are also available at major online book retailers.

Print information available on the last page.

ISBN: 978-1-4669-9945-9 (sc)
ISBN: 978-1-4669-9944-2 (e)

Library of Congress Control Number: 2013913720

Trafford rev. 04/11/2016

 www.trafford.com

North America & international
toll-free: 1 888 232 4444 (USA & Canada)
fax: 812 355 4082

Introduction

$\mathcal{U}$nderstanding what cancer is, how it begins and how it can become an entangled and life threatening growth is helpful knowledge that contributes toward preventing, containing, restraining and reducing the effects or even eliminating them; any or all depending on what degree of determination or commitment one decides to initiate in these efforts.

The power of wise, discretionary and unrelenting effort can bring satisfying results in the case of dealing with cancer or its potential as will be described.

Cancer has been recognized as being a threatening enemy and must be viewed in a very serious manner to prevent, maintain or especially win the battle against it whenever it occurs.

Similar views in this process of dealing with cancer will follow in the preface and are somewhat repetitiously articulated throughout the book for accentuating and retaining purposes.

Preface

*M*any books have been written about cancer and what can be done about it. This is another view of what its nature is, how to handle it and how it's destiny may unfold. Key factors of its destiny are either to accept it in its devastating manner that has led to terminal conditions, utilize new conventional methods to fight it or chase it out of our lives; all depending on how we choose to believe, approach and deal with it.

It's all a matter of acquired perception, attitude and determination. All three must be derived from broadly viewed information timely gained and coupled with new innovation.

The material herein is forwarded in a progressive manner that may influence the reader to better understand which route to choose when confronted with preventing, living with or eliminating cancer.

Not all people will believe there are better options than what they presently have, unfortunately, but the logical or positive type person knows there is always another way. That's what this book presents in its progressive entirety.

A certain amount of health history starts the progression that inevitably leads to options in dealing with cancer that may be referred to as rewards for the open minded. An open mind allows more room in venturing into helpful areas of whipping health problems. There is little room for expansion with an exploited and fixed mind other than more of the same.

Centuries and now approaching millenniums have been and are displaying outdated thoughts and beliefs which have been and are still limiting helpful and better resolutions particularly in philosophy, science and health.

The following views on preventing and eliminating cancer growths are dealt with in this progressive manner that allows the reader to better identify with realistic adaptations; not improvement through misleading stories, theories or fantasy. Also, one doesn't need a college degree to understand the following chapters. They are described in fairly plane language with a few technical terms.

These scripts unfold directly from your author who has lived a long life of health problems, health study and practice as a result of them. That study and practice has allowed your author an ability to conquer those ills through natural allowances, determination and a developed system of belief without surgery or conventional medicine for the most part.

This presentation of cancer is based on knowledge earned, practiced personally and shared with friends and relatives that has resulted in preventing, resisting, remitting and eliminating cancer cell mutation with them and your author.

Your author will be talking directly to you the reader with the use of the word "I" occasionally for relating personal views and experiences in this specific subject of cancer. Other views on retaining and improving health of mind and body are displayed in your authors many books listed after the end of these chapters.

The alternate reasoning for the contents of this book is to alert the individual reading it to help reduce fears of cancer and gain more knowledge of it for the purpose of controlling it within, help others to control it, live better with it, prevent it, put it in remission and/or eliminate it depending on what route one may learn to choose, believe and pursue.

The following chapters are comprised of priceless and personal experiences learned from the hard "knocks of life" and the availability of our great educational system in the area of health consciousness and its practices.

This book is primarily focused on developing cancer resistance and stopping it in natural oriented manners.

The foregoing chapters must not be considered as absolute advice or cure for any disease or illness because the possibilities of those assumptions, as in any other scripts pertaining to health and psychology for long life may not unfold exactly as the information is described or intended.

Also, your author herein informs the readers of not being a certified health care practitioner and does not misleadingly claim to be. The contents of this book is offered to help the readers make their own decisions concerning the following approaches toward dealing with cancer.

Your author's purpose is to be, primarily, an effective writer who offers people an opportunity to relax reading material that may add toward developing their own cause in whatever literary subject may be offered. Again, your author prefers the philosophy and approaches in overcoming illness in more of a natural manner, but realizes that is only a choice arrived at and not a declaration of the "only way."

My whole life has been one of health consciousness, study of it and practice for overcoming illness psychologically and physically for myself and others so I may be an example for those who wish to follow the accomplishments I have earned in this area of health for long life as is in many ways relative to my other books listed on health for long life.

Acquiring flexibility to as many options as possible is a meaningful and creative key toward maintaining or preventing cancer. These scripts are offered for expanding perspective in that area of health.

Contents

Chapter 1

Understanding what cancer is

$\mathcal{T}$he term cancer has been gathering a synonymous relationship with fear, gloom and shattered dreams in recent times with the sped up progress of increasing population and technological advancements.

Appearances are the more of everything humans have brought into the population, the more cancer has followed.

We need to understand what has been creepingly unfolding in this area of deteriorating health. Cancer can appear like some sort of new monster taking over our livelihood or at least seriously disturbing it in a way that alters the normal course of life.

Cancer not only attacks ill supported bodies of humans and animals, it also attacks young and healthy appearing life as though there are no exceptions to the appetite of this very misunderstood disease.

Does anyone ever ask, "What is it?" Very few. Not many ever care to talk about it. Do doctors tell anyone what it is? Very few. They only tell you indistinctly what it does when you get it, what your treatments are and/or estimate how long you will live, generally.

Anything not known is a mystery and anxiety accompanies mystery; hence fear forms and leads many to avoid being examined either periodically or upon noticeable symptoms. Literature is available on the subject, but who takes time to read about such a subject?

Had everyone been educated on what cancer is at a young age, they would be more inclined to embrace it as a normal function and react in a calm and objective manner to offset and/or eliminate the problem. Being educationally aware of what originally caused the action allows one to curb the mutation (growing) process before it extends its growth.

Cancer is better off viewed not as a creeping crud or invading foreigner, but as an opportunist which is there to dominate any weakened state of any protoplasmic life form of which is not always visible or even felt.

Four reasons why a cell does what it does: #1, it becomes disturbed. #2, it has formed a habit, #3, it is being reprogrammed and #4, it has a tendency to dominate other cells. This reasoning why a cell performs as it does is of a hypothetically psychological nature of which has not yet been discovered. Someday we may be able to psychoanalyze a body cell and understand them better. Temporarily, we only deal with what they do.

Cancer is a general term for specific body cell domination adversely affecting other cells and is referred to as having become cancerous or carcinogenic.

There are many views as to how cancer forms. Here are two others: #1. Our bodies are made up of billions of cells; white and red. Cancer is the name of what happens in body cells which become overwhelmingly subdued by other cells which have become overactivated and apparently confused by an abnormal body function. Appearances indicate a particular group of body cells engage in a nebulous panic as a result of either a constant infection, an incompatible body chemistry (mixture) due to various allergy reactions or other cancer causing factors explained in various ways as these scriptures unfold.

Those normal cells became disenchanted and strayed off their usual course and routine while carcinogenic initiators (adversely contributing toxically infested influences) cause oncogenes to activate. Other factors of tumor suppressors cause genes to become inactive. Then, normal cells become cancer dominated (sick, infected cells) like a constant meal.

Most body cells exist in routine and calmness. Certain groups of cells in the body become upset and disarrayed from elements and conditions which are not usual. Our cells are everywhere in our body system and it isn't terribly unusual for them to become upset, change form and move around to other areas. Why?

The body cells only know what to "do" from there inherited habits and the way the body's mind drives the individual's daily habits. When conflict exists in "usual" habits, those upset cells move accordingly in relationship with the individual's disarrayed conflicts. The conflicts can be anything as a combination of genetical calmness and present life's overexcitement or a genitical inheritance of excitement combined with present life's calmness. Many combinations cause conflict.

#2 of how cancer forms: The body cells only act and react instinctively according to influential strength from the "usual" and/or changing program.

Programming is the automatic direction from the unconscious mind to all the body cells. Occasionally the mind gets off balanced, derailed, out of whack or whatever and the body cells trail in their own manner. It's like a person lost in the wild without food or water. Survival is probable, but miserable. The same applies with cancer. The confused and habit derailed cells, either alone in their group or accompanied by other influences mentioned throughout this book, become sarcomatously, carcinomatosisly or lymphomasly infested (cancer initiation beginning). One might say they reach out and cling to anything and anything can be more desperation causing more of the same spread until they are all starved of their energies for survival. That's where we come in if our T cells aren't doing their job. We can choose our method of correcting the problem.

All cells are originally healthy. Influencing factors have weakened some in specific areas and they became victims of enzymatic infestation (the quiet normal cells that transform into factor formed cancer) which in turn become a spreading cycle called metastasis if allowed to continue. If not, #1, medical treatments are applied which usually destroys "all" the surrounding cells, nerves, and other essentials or surgery that removes a whole organ or more and possibly a surrounding area. #2, drugs are administered that usually deadens the pain or disguises the effects. #3, is where one refuses medical or surgical treatment with preferences of purposely applied natural methods reducing and eliminating the growths or #4, if no change is made in the growth area, the worse case scenario is where the metastasis continues throughout the body until fully consumed and death occurs if not treated properly.

Cancer is a matter of sick cells contaminating weaker cells. Resistance of lymphocyte T cells fight back or the affected person builds up body "and" mind resistance which is an alternative method and emphasized in this book.

Body cell activity is fastenating when viewing it as being necessary for sustaining life or it can add toward an environment capable of ending life through its undirected efforts which are overdue in changing cancer mutation.

The body can also put its protector T cells into action, if strong enough, curtailing the cancer and reduce it to a state of remission which means it stops its forward motion.

Infested cancer cells in remission still lingers with its potential until a time when a disciplined program of detoxifying is secured and cell purity is maintained.

Amazement never ends in stopping its forward motion with so many body cells interacting compatibly in one entity. However, just as billions of people appear somewhat compatible with one another, there are those who will detect or "smell" opportunities to "feed" or capitalize on weaknesses or supply of others. Resistance to utilizing these opportunities is also available just as are the opportunities. When man's T cells are strong enough, cells with cancer tendencies know they cannot successfully "charge in" and conquer, so they just continue doing what they were programmed for as entity neighbors. It's all about the age old saying and theory of the strong surviving or the "survival of the fittest." In this case, the masses together are the strongest when affectively joined.

All things being originally natural, living beings were and to some extent still are naturally protected against neighboring cell interference by our protector cells. The more recent advent of accelerated human progress has led to unnatural stress and toxic infiltration which has reduced protoplasmic protectibility (the T cells designed to fight off the trouble making cells).

Cancer deformity and illness is now generally "hanging" at the mercy of treatment initiated by conventional medicine and surgery influenced and guided by insurance companies. Their objectives are, primarily, to rid the affected area of accosting and accosted cells by eradicating them and the area if necessary.

Modern cancer isn't much different than it was thousands of years ago basically. There is just more of it now with more people and there are more misplaced toxins and genetically cultured tendencies which have added to multiply reasons for its obvious threat in maintaining natural body integrity.

The process of cancer is one function. The word cancer is a misunderstood representative showering indications of ugliness, fear, weakness, conglomerate control over and negative feedback programming of inevitable death plus the energy draining state of anxiety one is so accustomed to falling into when told, "You have cancer."

The process of cancer is what most of mankind believes is a type of out of control incompatibility with nature. It is a belief of lacking control and prompts mankind to kill it; mostly because of dealing with it as though it were an incorrigible foreigner from outer space similar to some of these movies where the army is summoned to kill the invaders from outer space.

Cancer, for the benefit of preventing cell migration, consumption and mistreatment must be further and continuously viewed as a part of our influenced or newly learned mind and body programming, not as a thing of which we have no control over. Further chapters will shed light on this view. It can, is and/or will be considered a normal migration of which can positively diminish as well as negatively expand.

The chapters will unfold with more on what to do about cancer as we proceed.

Cancer is "not" an unstoppable disease. It only grows with the continued support that made it begin and will slow down or stop growing when the source is reduced or alleviated. What is a little complicated is determining which factors contributed the most and which consecutively contributed less.

Understanding how we acquire cancer growth is so relatively close to understanding how to eliminate it. Societies around the world have missed the simplicities of understanding it better. One might say those societies of multimillions have had entirely too much data of too many different desires wanting everything their own way.

Sure, there has been a lot of very good progress in the supposed advancements of science for health, but they could have shortened the time and stressful confusion of that progress had they proceeded with and continued procedures of wholistic and natural oriented health. Watch.

Understanding our inherited tendencies isn't too difficult and could have been, as it can now, utilized for parents training their children from birth to only live where there is only clean and fresh water, then to eat and drink pure food and liquid. Next, train them to prevent situations that create stress, worry, illness and social complications and misery. Last, train them to program their minds for survival purposes which means focusing more on remaining healthy for a better life amongst one another. That manner of basics will travel wide and "maybe" circulate around to everyone. Those following months and years will, in turn, result in more natural, pure and healthier societies capable of curtailing excessive chemical, social and psychological toxins which adds so many more deterioration oriented influences supporting cancer among other self-inflicted diseases. We have the power to change it. Choosing to exercise initiating it is all it takes. We "can" do it. Putting our children in better environment too hard to do? Planning ahead in having those kids would sure make it a lot easier. Education for that planning will solve that problem. That requires more people to become more interested in this subject.

Business conglomerates can make just as much money promoting natural methods as compared to drugs and surgery and be much more appreciated while contributing to a better world for all. Medical and wholistic healthcare must eventually merge. Why not now?

Once again, cancer isn't generally some kind of invader from outside our bodies. It is our "own" body cells which became adversely affected by genetic influence and/or toxic exposure and consumption. This must be more thoroughly understood for managing cancer situations.

Cancer "is" caused by many inside and outside our body factors. It is our individual responsibility or added help from others to gain knowledge of those influencing factors and offset them as leverage to prevent, starve or lesson the surge of deteriorating cancer cells.

Chapter 2

Why is it so important to understand what cancer is?

$\mathcal{D}$ecades and generations now going into centuries have left a profound effect of fear in the hearts of humans concerning how devastating cancer can be. Many such incidents of cancer plague have, instead of preventing it, actually accented it and stimulated the growth by avoiding the realities of it; pro and con. Being more realistic about it will help.

Personal experiences of cancer cases, fear oriented and negative gloom and doom talk about cancer and even the educational system of gory details concerning cancer hasn't exactly set good examples or a bright outlook concerning future concepts of where cancer is headed let alone how to more effectively manage it and at the same time decrease its momentum, reverse it or even eliminate it completely and concentrate on something meaningful.

The only power solutions available now are led by medical doctors, hospitals and insurance companies as said, certainly not near as many wholistic practitioners or individuals accepting responsibility for their own actions and reactions of disease such as cancer.

People around the civilized part of the world have almost always been exploited to follow and believe what conglomerate institutions tell them concerning state of leadership, state of mind, religious consciousness and health among a few other basics. Reacting to cancer discovery and management isn't much different. People tend to believe what they are told, more than not, without much questioning.

Thoroughly understanding any subject for better results requires a little more probing. It seems logical a potentially life threatening disease warrants better understanding before proceeding with any analysis, assistance, guidance or possible resolution for offsetting or eliminating the problem; cancer in this case.

Understanding how older people develop cancer is fairly widespread knowledge, but how little kids with seemingly uncontaminated new bodies and good health get it isn't clear to most observers. That's where understanding more becomes necessary to deal with it in a cool, calm, patient, objective and effective manner for lasting purposes, not just for gaining a little more time of life when it became too late to treat.

If long or longer life is not an objective goal, understanding cancer may not be so important. However, common statistics indicate life sustainment is high in demand and expectations. So, generally, knowing more of the gory details along with gaining an optimistic view largely supporting the method of reducing the effects "and" the worrisome anxiety associated with cancer allows one to appreciate understanding cancer better. Then, choices of proceeding to prevent or reduce the cancer growth will be more favorable and one will be "on course" in preventing or reducing the processing cancer infestation.

The importance of understanding cancer also means one will look into options bringing cancer growth to a point of stopping which usually means, #1 some type of surgery that cuts something out or off or #2, a wholistic approach without surgery or other medical treatments. This is what I call part of boiling it down to what is important.

Surgery and or prescription drugs are established as being right and proper by the institutions which have initiated and supported that particular philosophy. It has all come together through established rules, righteousness and profits.

The natural or wholistic approach is also a philosophy of further and different methods of offsetting and dealing with cancer growth in contrast to the medical manners. Sometimes they "tend" to agree and "do" have similar options.

One must know the difference between the two and surely must not just take a chance on one of them. They are both practiced around the world. They both have some spectacularly good results. They must both be checked out. After all, like they say, we only have one life of how we are at present. Choosing the best methods we think we can support and live with is what we are striving for in this book.

I view procedures of cancer correction and reduction as follows: Medical examinations are state of the art and totally needed in specific areas while wholistic approach in most cases unfold with excellent and philosophically natural methods. I like to keep all my body parts. More on these procedures in further chapters.

Cancer is basically a process of sickened body cells spreading to other cells until organ function ceases to exist if not checked, treated or stopped.

Specific cancer varies as the following examples state:

#1. Genetically influenced cancer: The term genetic is also misunderstood to be an absolute followup of ancestral cell descendancy. That is not exactly fitting in all cases. There are some inherited facsimiles, but most of the so called genetic transfer can be of a cultural tendency embedded in the living being cells influenced by immediate family, friends and associates; even the affected cancer cells. That may explain why some cancer cells are more aggressive in their approach than others where some of the parent inheritance passed down freshly influenced traits. Maybe it's time to start training the parents to cool down and train the body cells to stay healthy.

#2. Programmed cancer: Human programming can be culturally, accidentally or deliberately cultivated for any reason. When the programming becomes vested and takes effect (all through the cell structure), the cancer cells are also affected in a similar manner. When the affected cells become malignant cancer cells, they do it in such a manner as the whole body and mind is programmed. If it is passive programming, the mutation time may be slow. If it is aggressive, the mutation time may be much quicker. Programming can be environmentally influenced, not necessarily self-inflicted from the individual. There is more toxin exposure now than ever.

#3. Virus cancer: This type of cancer is usually thought of as a foreign disease intering from something or someone else looking for a meal. Again, this is sometimes very misunderstood. This disease may have been lingering in the bloodstream and became active with and in the cancer cells. However, in view it attacks the body's cells leaving an effect on the cancer cells within the body, it has been customarily referred to as virus cancer. When body weakness is known, virus attacks may be more beneficially managed by a professional in this area. Virus cancer is still a subject in question.

Since a virus cannot be efficiently controlled by the mind as any other self-inflicted disease can, it is more effectively treated with the use of drugs, herbs, supplements and immune system support. One of them, a combination of them or even all of them may be utilized as options depending on the direction of the person's decision who is responsibly "in charge" of that condition.

The prementioned examples are expressed only to support the importance of understanding cancer better for dealing with it. Individual incapability usually warrants the assistance and/or guidance of a certified health care practitioner (medical or wholistic) when confronted with any cancerous situation or having interest in preventing or combating it.

Cancer has been historically thought of as some kind of mysterious monster that devours the body and mind of humans. Why only humans? Domestic animals have suffered from it too. Prior to early medicine, it was thought in worst scenario views. It may not have been called cancer, but they all passed down evil consciousness of what they saw and evaluated when referring to the disease we now call cancer.

Many cases of this disease, as with other unpleasant appearing illness, were treated similarly to those who were sent to leper colonies and left to wither and die. If they looked bad, they sent them away.

Updating the changing progress on cancer, more has been observed, studied and researched for benefits of adding toward placing cancer to rest as time passes. Now we are much less afraid of a disease we understand more and no one now would even "think" of hiding or doing away with an inflicted victim of cancer. Now, we join in challenging cancer's potentiality for eliminating it through more understanding of it. Cheers for adding to the purpose of reducing cancer to function much less horrendously than in the past. Generally, we are pointed in that direction. We just need more confidence and belief of being able to handle the disease especially before it handles us. That, of course, means we need to have the knowledge necessary for understanding it and to prevent it transforming from weak or adversely existing cells to sick cells.

Understanding cancer is easy to say or suggest, but maybe not so easy to gather and retain, right? The other side of the coin of understanding it is worth the effort applied because understanding cancer allows one to understand many other illnesses for the benefit of offsetting or conquering. Diet, genetics and way of life kind of simplifies it. That shouldn't be too hard to retain basically. Just fill in a few details which are in this book for the layman or anyone else desiring other views on the subject and the importance of understanding cancer will become much clearer.

Chapter 3

How far back in history is cancer known?

$\mathscr{C}$ancer is believed to have invaded mankind and animals as far back as three to five thousand years.

The Chinese had different names and descriptions of it nearly five thousand years ago when it wasn't viewed as a carcinogenic disease and treated it in their wholistic manner and has been ever since. Not much new there except they have improved their methods along with modern influence.

Logical process of elimination indicates when we travel back in time to the beginning of mankind (the scientific view, that is) when their cellular viscera and visceral (organs etc.) were formed, they were vulnerable to other competing neighbors who also had needs like the lions consuming the antelopes etc. This logic only reveals animals consume animals and cells consume cells.

We may think cancer growth is relatively new. Alas, present day phenomena are only copies carried down through the long eras of time. People with multiple, diverse and dissimilar cell life including cancer cells are basic as they were much prior to the history of language. Using the logic of elimination, basic biology has been proven to follow for multimillions of years as the alligators, turtles, rodents etc. have remained the same. So do the body's cells; mostly.

Needless to say, there was no illness concepts or names to the self-inflicted diseases in that far away period of time and no passed down history except for those in more recent millenniums.

Who cares how far back it goes? We all better start caring a lot more! Caring more about the past is the philosophical key that will open many doors toward knowing more how to progressively leave the past with all its unsupported problems causing endless pangs and stumbling of human progress.

If no one cares about the past, no one will care about yesterday or one hour ago. We can easily nail it down to now and that can bubble over into the future; so watch it!

Known cancer, as the chapter title questions, descends to records on old scrolls, blocks of rock, in mountain caves and on other crude material on ancient discovered cadavers. The evidence doesn't exactly spell the word cancer in most cases when we are talking about millenniums past, but the evidence of deterioration tells enough to fairly assume ancient death occurred from progressive swelling and their complications leaving residual evidence in a preserved environment of systematic metastasis. That type of evidence allows researchers to trace further DNA evidence of which determines age at death, lifestyle and faults during life and at death.

Lifestyle of ancient cadavers tells a lot about how societies and nomads lived. That, in turn, reveals lengths of time specific diseases existed. Fortunately for the mentioned scrolls and notes scribed on crude material, science has determined approximate time periods cancer has been active.

The word cancer, originally referred to astrological concepts and beliefs. Applying that term to disease began later when early European medical men observed and researched common tumors which inevitably revealed carcinoma malignancy, which was discovered to be various types of progressive cancer action and an eventual term of cancer was adopted to separate the difference between tumors of nonlife threatening and life threatening conditions.

Cancer, it seems fair to say from calculating its three thousand years of gathered data plus ancient cadaver inspection probably descends much longer than that. However, the possibility of cancer's potential being life threatening then is not logically favorable because artificial toxins and accelerated stress etc. were undoubtedly less the further back in time we go. It is an amazing paradox, though, where we now live in an age when we have access to more of everything to solve problems than ever and yet we are also confronted with surmountingly more health problems than ever. True, we are whipping a lot of it, but with more people than ever, there is more volume of self-inflicted disease including cancer.

It is totally necessary to become scared out of our seats to realize mankind can become extinct not because of cancer. That's only one problem, but because we have caused too many health and environment problems in our realm of nature with overpopulation, greed and indifference gathered on the way. The rate we are moving ahead with chemical products, greed, overpopulation, consuming toxins and indifference will create a giant cancer of many differences that will dwarf all our present health problems put together and render us extinctly out of common humanity into a slowly, squeezing society of robotic type mummies before the end.

Let's pay more attention to what nature has always offered us even way before the advent of conventional religion which is to utilize our natural powers of personal spirituality, wholistic approaches and what amounts to the golden rule for reducing our world to a more philosophically, healthier and perspectively caring place as compared to a most progressively chaotic venture into nowhere. Cancer is only a minute part of it all now, but can add toward a conglomeration of possibly irreversal disease. We "can" turn it all around by first turning it down.

There will be more on natural procedure unfolding in further chapters ahead.

Ironically speaking in view of medical/surgical takeover in these technological times, natural procedure is nothing new or unheard of. It was here first and a mighty long time prior to these modern days. Identifying with it can be very "natural." It certainly doesn't mean we have to reverse all our accumulated options in the health care "industry," if you will. It just means we can carry forward all the wisdom we can acquire "from" the past and integrate what will be most beneficial to the cause of our present "and" future without putting profit first.

Mankind has very slowly developed these commonly experienced diseases of cancer, atherosclerosis and diabetes etc. over an evolutionary period of time propagated equally by the oncoming advents of human achievement. Paradoxically, we have created a destiny where the ongoing progress of immensely spectacular change has trailed with growing side effects as these self-inflicted diseases. It almost seems like building an endless tower only to tumble. Let's change it.

Our progress with the trailing side effects can be curtailed with the adverse experiences along the way up. It just seems mankind isn't too interested in getting serious about leveling off or even stopping the tower of progress for adjusting to another plane of insight. This is needed for that overdue cancer curtailing. Let's get serious.

Nature is patiently standing by to assist in revitalizing new views and approaches to preventing a tower of progress to fall, crumble or even worse; struggle in the progress of furthering its cause. It is something to think about.

How long cancer has been known isn't really the whole issue. Cancer is only part of the effects of progressive circumstances. The important aspect of the progression is how much worse will we let this obvious tower of progress continue on its present path before "everything" gets worse in health of body and mind combined with our social, industrial and environmental dilemmas and population expansion?

The importance of cancer's past is what has unfolded in that area over a long period of time. We can get an idea, perspectively, how it matured into a worldwide plague of misery that only became worse with the advent of time and more people.

Now, with that historical hindsight, we can reasonably assume it will continue its habitual course into more of the future maybe at its present rate of maturity unless curtailed because of what we might term as its popular demand. Yes, popular demand is described here as ignorant indulgences which have contributed toward cancer of our close people as well as the eventuality of the increasing masses of those people who do not understand cancer.

History is dictating a necessity to reduce the inevitable cancer conquest of mankind with newly developing health methods of which may be the only humane manner available. This book explains them some in specific and some in general contexts.

Moving ahead, we must first individually change our ways based on what we have seen from the past so future generations and centuries etc. will view the past turnaround as meaningful progress for survival. This is what we are doing in these studies.

Now the progress of resolving the creeping symptoms of cancer are being contained mostly by medical procedure with their accepted results and terms associated with their affiliate insurance companies. Wholistic practices are on the rise with increasingly good results as individuals are assuming more responsibility for their condition. The race and competition between the two aggregates of power to dominate the health industry will somewhat calm cancer down until the population is reduced. Then we will experience much better results.

We are now at the head of the helm for grasping a hold onto the cancer situation for controlling it and our destiny of health. Upcoming books by your author will explain more on our population dilemma which needs even more attention for our survival.

Chapter 4

Who are potential candidates for cancer?

$\mathcal{C}$ancer has been on the upswing as mankind has progressed mostly through recent centuries. The more modern we have become, the more exotic pleasures we have adapted with which means varying from the norm of our natural environment to smokestacks and industrial air circulation, artificial fertilizer, food preservatives, domestic and commercial stress, ignoring health maintenance, filling the mind with excessive money making activity, spending money on pleasures and scrimping on nutrients necessary for combating these modern influences contributing toward quietly creeping diseases etc., etc. These are only examples of reasons why progressive change over the centuries has affected health resistance of our people in what appears to have been an increasing trend of, in this case, cancer. Believe it, cancer creeps in many different ways.

Millenniums of years ago to more recent time of centuries, men were tough. They walked and ran across the lands, rode animals and sailed in rickety boats with tougher men oaring them. The woman were tough too. They were hard workers and didn't complain. If they did, it was because of what the men didn't do.

Self-inflicted disease wasn't rampant in those era's of time. Air and water everywhere was pure. Food was natural and the future was so clear, one could see through it. Now, it's so dense, misleading and vague, one has to exertly strive to maintain optimistic goals and hope they will be lucky enough to see their goals realized either for a while or even in their lifetime. Cynical view? Maybe, with all things considered. We all need to offset our present attitudes where all is turning sour and nothing good is happening in the world. That thinking becomes believing and that believing makes it happen all the more. These timely and overpowering changes tend to saturate the psyche when continued and habitually creates more of the same. Everything strong or weak being basically relative to change, cancer dominance isn't much different.

Retrospectively speaking when cancer wasn't publicly highlighted; genetic, toxic and psychological influence quietly existed and was creating various cell deterioration including carcinoma growths from its cell domination. People and animals too lived and died with it without much societal ado. Only the advent of time reoccurrence brought expanded consciousness of the growing nuisance and eventually became a national and international health pandemic whirling science into panic probing where cancer became a challenge to conquer as a number two most life threatening disease.

Heart disease never really created a panic type reaction across the globe because it was always pretty much accepted as a normal way to die; of the heart failing to beat plus there wasn't much visible change noticed in the person's deterioration. Cancer, on the other hand, had very scary indications with swelling, shrinking, bleeding and infectious ugliness. Those appearances and suffering sparked negative reactions into the hearts of human responses.

The progress of animal cancer was less intense or progressive since most everyone was incapable of understanding it, expressing an emotion of panic or being alert to change it.

Humans have always overreacted to anything abnormal, fearful or threatening. Cancer has caused all three of them.

Individual vulnerability to cancer in humans vary, now we know, due to their lifestyle, diet, climate, air quality, genetic influence, employment and social pressure, emotional and biological strength, rearing and chemical exposure to mention a few. That indicates almost everyone is a candidate for cancer. The exception of those are people who steadily maintain consciousness of those conditions which add toward the transmutation of body cells known as cancer and purposely regulate their life style for improving and better health habits.

A world of change in individuals can change a world of desperately needed changes. Contagious disease alarms people to make changes. Individual changes pertaining to self-inflicted disease such as cancer can also be helpfully contagious and spread through the realm of cancer consciousness revealing and creating better prevention and cure methods for the disease. Eventually, there will be less "candidates" because of the diminishing cases of cancer. The potential for individuals or populations being directly or indirectly vulnerable to the disease of cancer is rationally displayed here as being somewhat relatively equal to that of the substance input of the contributions mankind has created toward that disease. That substance (same old story) is the combination of contributing factors which has, is and still will cause cancer. They have been mentioned and will be further extrapolated in this book.

Reducing the odds of candidacy is in the hands of #1, the individual depending on one's openness, power and ability to flex with belief, adaptability and determination to begin and remain focused on proven methods of natural and more rewarding approach of preventing and/or managing cancer. Reducing those odds are also in the hands of #2, the overall masses of people who practice the same as #1 which is to say: Everything meaningful starts with one person being successful and that's great for that one person. What a pity and waste of potential, though, for it to be limited to only one. The ultimate in human value and meaningful value is for everyone reaping the harvest of naturally increased health through the combined power of mutual effort.

Mutual effect will be more realized as one has completed this book and begins more practice with wholistic methods and spreads the word of vitalizing and revitalizing old and new methods of bringing one back to normal from the vacuum of cancer and its affects.

The more people are convinced cancer can be handled better by natural and wholistic methods, the more other people will adapt to it by watching, listening and beginning natural methods. The people of this world "want" to live and they are beginning to realize, more than ever, that which maintains better health attributes to longer life. They just need a little reminding once in a while.

Momentum can work against us or it can work with us in conquering cancer among other self-inflicted disease. It can drag us down with it by doping, slicing or chopping while not educating any other way or we can ascend into an opportune time of prevention and natural methods which will allow us to feel better, more confident and happier because of our efforts and knowledge of there being more alive future.

After all is said and probed, seems as though the potential candidates for cancer would be those who are either not informed of options for disease control, those who ignore methods to prevent them or those who have enough knowledge, but are too busy to be serious about dealing or caring to deal with cancer, its causes, its victims or even with the potential threat to the self.

We could surmise a pretty long list of candidates for cancer just by looking at what lifestyles people are living. They "think" they are okay within their circles and environment. That "thinking" is more like a wild guess. Influential factors promulgating cancer mutation are gathering more everyday while the world's population is closing in with the passage of time.

I, your author thought I would never be a victim of cancer. Low and behold, what a slapping surprise when I was told I had it. I let my guard down with prevention discipline for awhile and that's what happened. However, now I am slowly boiling it way down through methods mentioned in this book.

Some of us tend to be candidates for cancer and have to wrestle with it. Let's wrestle to win! It works.

There is a theory traveling around in the health scene when cancer is gone, it can return because of the aging process. This may be true when one doesn't offset that theory by practicing preventive methods. The aging process unfolds on an average of self-sustaining maintenance. Of course that process can be propagated in many different ways depending on individual choice of options. Maintaining strict health habits generally slows the aging process down. There are many paths to that goal. Not practicing them defeats that theory. Sorry about that. We are only potential candidates for cancer if we allow it to form. That's how serious we need to view it. Let's view it with strength of mind, determination, optimism, respect of being humble, flexible and open, but without fear.

Since politics appears to have dominated the term candidate where one seeks, qualifies or is in some cases, destined to fit the job, more consciousness of the word is attracting candidacy relating to other cases such as the potential destiny of acquired cancer development. Nowadays, a person can be more readily recognized as being a "candidate" for cancer by noticing the lifestyle of negative health habits, environmental exposure and inherited influences from family traditions which will all tell a lot about what adds to the attraction of attacking cells forming cancer. It's something to seriously prepare for ahead of being stricken so the doctors won't have to unleash any unfavorable news.

Chapter 5

What is cancer's destiny?

$\mathcal{A}$ strologically, cancer's destiny will probably last as long as humanity does. Some of mankind's beliefs and habits aren't very susceptible to change even if it does mean an opportunity to improve or flex with inevitable variations brought on by other changes. Human tendencies are very strong. By the same token, they can lift us out of a gloom and doom syndrome.

Health deterioration, including cancer before it had a name, lingered in the societies of mankind as just one of the illnesses that led to old age and death without realizing what it's destiny was other than a miserable end of life.

Ancient man lived simple, uncomplicated and uncontaminated lives compared to the paradoxical traps they later put themselves into in their accidental and more deliberate schemes to grow and progress as with having more children thereby contributing to the destiny of accelerating "needs." That, in turn, required them to accelerate further with those needs while developing their spirituality to get more of what they wanted. They took what they wanted by ignoring any sense of spirituality. All of this added to greed of which they denied and justified as "good business."

Paradoxically and with the very thing they thought would make them happy and reasonably contented similarly to their prehistorically uncomplicated existence, their relentless efforts in acquiring those dreams have still desecratively vanished through self-indulgence.

Cancer isn't "just" a disease. It is incidentally conglomerated fallout of psychobiological infiltration caused by conflict with human desire, ambition and their pretentious collisions with nature's anciently fixed stances. That is to say, one will win and one will lose. Who is in charge of winning and what is better to win over; things, people or "the self?"

Cancer has been "picked up" or established by human destiny's tendencies to rule aside "and" within natures destiny. That combination doesn't work too well. One works better.

Now, human conflicts with endlessly complicated chemical substances also add to the direction of cancer's conquest and destiny. This is the human relationship with cancer at present.

The progresses of world societies have placed themselves in positions of conflict with nature and it has effected many areas of these psycho and biological functions; in this case, the life supporting chemistry of body cell survival.

Humans are leading the way in their foolish mannerism of supplying "stuff" for their survival. They are going about it in what they refer to as a "moving forward" manner when in actuality they are, again, paradoxically and systematically eliminating human and animal life on planet Earth. Scary? Sure it is philosophically. Just remember, though, humans primarily care for things pertaining to now. We hear them saying, "All there is is now" on a regular basis. True, they talk about the future of their grand kids, but you don't hear the grand kids complaining. Each generation seems to be able to accept the conditions they were born into. Each generation picked up actual manners of living from past generations because they seemed reasonably comfortable and it continues on. Time passed and big incidences become bigger like climate change and incurable disease. How about super government control over "all" the people?" Disease comes in many forms. It creeps in until someone attempts to stop it and wins or loses.

Cancer disease, if you will plus others, is conceptually similar where the cell activity "moving forward" changes too. It keeps science researchers, polititions, insurance companies and patients on the hot seat in their attempts to determine which route to approach in at least offsetting the surprising and confusing transmutation of especially self-inflicted disease. That could and can be very well managed by the self for longer term health through wholistic methods. Temporary "cures" of drugs and surgery do not appear to be designed for the benefit of living a longer life than what is considered normal.

Cancer cells are like people. They are receptors of our brain and tend to respond to how our brain is programmed mostly and some by our environmental influence which contributes to that programming. Our environment is the sum total of all our influences, society's "and" Earth's materials and atmosphere. This "is" big and may be "too big" for any of us to handle. That's why the importance of becoming more conscious of changing our personal direction is necessary now more than ever. We have open opportunity to conquer growing self-inflicted disease (specifically cancer in this case) and direct its destiny toward being controlled by mankind instead of the disease.

Once self-inflicted disease is conquered, we will be acquiring more strengths to offset and possibly annihilate virus diseases by transforming them into useable protein or other workable substances as crazy as that sounds now.

The destiny of cancer is realistically in the palms of our hands as it unknowingly has been and now may continue to be. We are, theoretically, intelligently enough developed to guide ourselves along with cancer's destiny for managing and eliminating this nebulous nuisance of a disease as time passes. Let's give ourselves this necessary opportunity to do it with more of this kind of study and practice where and/or when needed or chosen.

We have all inherited some form of weakness in our body's circulatory system of which no one has really known why other than it is there. Some beliefs profess we are born perfect, but this disease acquired from weakness doesn't sound very perfect unless it means perfectly weak.

Without having a rational or provable response to the weakness contention indicating it may be somewhat valid, we are all in a position to speculate, point out, or purposely drive the destiny of cancer or any other self-inflicted disease away. The later of choices is more favorable by myself, your author, because accepting responsibility for "my" destiny, largely, is the soundest basis for creating the progress of my desires. If one has a firm belief in "God" as being the driver of destiny, then remember that famous old saying, "God helps those who help themselves." That combination can be equally fitting. Everyone has a choice. I know, that too is debatable for searching minds, not fixed minds. Those who do not allow room for other possibilities will not allow room in their minds for expanding their scope of intelligence, therefore become subjects of someone or something else and cannot or will not allow self-direction. If you are one of those, look out! You may not be allowing yourself to make any of your own decisions. If that's the case with the destiny of cancer, it will run your life. You will not allow yourself to run its life and I still say, you have the right to change that. I was given that birthright just from being born and "do" exercise it. Why not you too?

Narrowing the odds down for changing the course of cancer's destiny generally for everyone is, obviously, a big task for one person. However, one person can do wonders for that one person just by believing, thinking, adapting and practicing the wholistically natural way of prevention and/or elimination methods. Reducing the odds of cancer's destiny begins with the individual and spreads to others automatically changing the course of that destiny. It's in our hands to "lead" that destiny by exercising it and proving it to be meaningful, needed and rewarding. This timely "adds" to conventional methods.

Most societies of the world appear to understand destiny as being directed by a driving source of some spiritual nature. Since that concept of destiny is rarely discussed, there are also appearances which indicate those people aren't really sure about that spiritual theory because of the way they "do" make so many trillions of choices themselves creating that destiny.

If people live in fear of naming their own destiny such as a "make sense" destiny of conquering disease effects of cancer, then further appearances indicate they won't allow themselves to make any other decisions guiding or directing their destiny.

Living in fear to change and/or direct our life's health and survival exists as a contrary view to the spiritual contention we were all meant to live in perfect harmony with nature.

Actually, deciding to add to or take some away from our approach toward healthcare maintenance doesn't have to be such an earthshaking revelation unless one is so sternly bent on upholding what appears as very inflexible rules established in ancient times by very inflexible men who understood even in those days where rules would eventually have to change or break down; and they do.

Is all this probing rhetoric necessary just for questioning the destiny of cancer you ask? Nothing in the area of healthcare with everyone involved deserves to be overlooked especially when it pertains to dealing with what we can, will or won't believe in.

Let us not guess what we believe in. Let us be more reasonably confident in what we believe in. It's well worth the extra effort in supporting our destiny beside that of cancer's destiny.

Mankind either has the right or adopts the right to program how to lead the destiny of their lives "and" for how long. When practicing or adopting that course of responsibility, we must remain susceptibly open for the unending rewards of that encounter to guide it. Read your author's book "Paradox Of Destiny Explained" for comprehensive information on this subject.

Chapter 6

What is the worst and the best in cancer's progress?

$\mathcal{C}$ancer is evaluated here in two aspects for the worst and two aspects for the best. The first one is from the viewpoint of the affected cell which is about to speak: "The worst scenario I can think of as a cancer cell would be when mankind finally "realizes" the detrimental consequences of a power, glory and money oriented society that produces more children than they can substantially handle, more food grown in chemically manufactured fertilizer and more chemical drugs for manipulating illnesses or creating euphoric imagery. They also swelter and mar one's immune system with industrial and auto emissions, and deceives the public causing self-inflicted disease and many other health hindrances galore to say nothing of destructive effects of alcohol drinking and tobacco smoking. The second worst aspect for me is when mankind finally grabs the reigns of control to slow the disease programmed cells down in all aspects of life on Earth (not just body cells) and begins learning, practicing and promoting the process of embracing natural methods of living as much as they can after centuries of astrayed results. I, as a cancer cell, will slowly fade away into remission and I will no longer have the chance to spread the disease. Poor me. That's the worst that can happen to me; a self-inflicted cancer disease maker. Actually, I as a cancer producing cell, "am" a significant part of what seems normal to me at the time of my reign of terror and would surely feel devastated without my job."

The first aspect of cancer's progress is, of course, from the viewpoint of the stricken individual. What could be worse if that person was an unsuspecting victim? First would be the initial shock of being diagnosed with this spooky thing called cancer (in this case, spooky means not knowing anything about it other than it spreads ugliness and can cause pain and possibly death). That's scary and can actually add to the victim's vulnerability. The second worse in line would be when that person was told there was only six months or so left to live. Much less than that scare would be the options of treatments including state of the arts medical treatments which kills everything involved around the affected area including the healthy cells. It's like dropping an A bomb on the battlefield in a world which was once so naturally uncontaminated and meant to be as is.

Part of the second worse in line is surgery which extracts a whole area where cancer is busy. Once it has all been removed, there are no more choices unless it is to do it again at another time when, obviously, the lifestyle will probably continue in the same manner with a good chance of causing a repeated problem.

Of course the stricken victim is temporarily relieved. He or she just has to live on sheer hope of being cured from that point forward because of not being willing to change, use discipline or train the brain to prevent a reoccurrence of cancer. It's been said, "So I won't live a long life. I'm okay now and that's all that matters." More power to that attitude if that's what they choose.

Now let's view the best that can happen with the "progress" of cancer from the cancer cell followed by the victim.

First is the view from the cancer cell: "The best scenario of progress would be when I sense loads of toxins entering my sphere of cells coupled with a genetic gang of supporting relatives and friends jumping in with me for the feast. Then I know the world is going bananas with its health stability and are on the right course for my success in running the show of putrid health by my systematic methods of debilitation and causing a lot of chaotic misery in the human species of living beings. That's when we cancer cells really live it up in our process of spreading disease. Then, when they try to fix it, many times they make a worse mess out of it hacking, sawing, spurting blood and flesh all over. Sometimes, it sends me downstream to another area to start all over again. What a hayday! Sure, they may bludgeon us out of a job for awhile, but those humans are gluttons for pleasure, glory, fame and whatever makes lots of money. They almost guarantee me steady work.

Second best is the security where the human victims will, without too much doubt, repeat falling into their previous habits of indulgence and probably won't change their present health habits or their genetic programming which "is" possible, so I don't have a lot to worry about in loosing this excitingly rewarding job until they wake up. Since they still appear to exist in a fantasy where the progress of money and technology is "most" important while it is toxinizing society along with the usual methods which adds to that combination, I will work steady. That's second best for me!" End of cancer cells.

Now let's view the best that could happen from a victim of cancer infestation. While I your author am presently one of them in the recovery stage, the best scenario I can look forward to is becoming and staying focused on my steadfast belief where, while being influentially stricken by my opportunistic and covertly developed cancer cells, these cells are not foreign strangers to me. They are mine and even though I temporarily relaxed my guard and control over them by allowing toxic exposure and emotional instability to run a little wild, I have regained and improved my environmental, hygienic and emotional stability. While I remain in this status of mind, practice it, preach it and utilize my acquired natural and developed abilities for slowing and at the same time dissolving the effects of this negative cell transformation, I am gathering more knowledge, patience, understanding, determination and optimism in a definite reduction of cancer growth. The process is now slowing to normalcy notch by notch and I look forward to further and finally eliminating any balance of malignancy in my self-inflicted cancerous disease.

My second best progress with cancer is having had the opportunity of being touched with cancer which has allowed me to accept more responsibility of promoting its mutational descent along with feeling educationally optimistic about eliminating its action and being another example of that progress.

The personal experience I have had with cancer has become equally if not more valuable than my lifetime study of health and psychology of reports, school, circulars, doctors, books, seminars and TV documentaries etc.

By the way, I'm "not" promoting a product for selling to the public; only the various subject books I've written. I'm just a writer who has studied, experienced and learned enough to spread as good a word as possible that may help others in some way they may choose.

Finally, let me summarize a little broader view of the worst and the best that could happen in cancer's progress. We see now, that progress seems to persist in producing cancer infiltration or eliminating it completely. Gaining more awareness of both is what we are doing now. Progress is progress; good or bad! If we choose to turn our heads and display little or no interest in the permanency of this varment, that will inevitably unfold as continuously worse in the scenario. Worse things have had a way of creeping up on us. Then, either panic or desperation sets in of which seldom improves much of anything at the time.

The other side of the coin, if you will, is an optimistic, responsible and maybe even energetic view where we the people individually, if not supported by business and political conglomerates, can whip cancer completely by a few who choose that route or by the masses who go wholistic. That few or masses will name cancer's progress or destiny by declaring action, commitment, belief and practice toward its elimination. That's the best that can happen when the momentum increases. Nothing will stop it the same as defeated diseases of the past.

The defeated diseases of the past are reminders where mankind is the ultimate in conquering anything conquerable. We have come an immensely long way in proving just how good we are at conquering things of mystery and far fetched wonders. No other species of living beings have extended themselves out reaching for the stars as mankind has and we will continue to do so as long as we are alive and striving.

We have seen the worst and the best of nature and of our accomplishments and we will see many more of them because that is the destiny so many of us have strived for.

We are, at present, experiencing a movement of transition from an ongoing worst situation in cancer to an oncoming best situation in reducing cancer. This book is just an instrument for stimulating overdue changes which is to bring out the best in cancer progress from the view point of mankind's challenges. The best of cancer's progress is on its way through our determination and nothing will stop it. That progress is traveling through this book and out through the efforts of all the participants of cancer prevention and elimination with efforts of the old, the present and the new manners of approach.

Becoming aware of the worst in cancer isn't something to avoid looking at by turning one's head away or ignoring the possibilities. That just shuts off any possible education of which could be immensely helpful if and/or when one either chooses preventive methods or is faced with the need to rid one's self of cancer.

The cost of ignoring those possibilities of acquiring cancer isn't worth it. Remaining open pays more than one may realize. May the best decision and approach lead the way.

Chapter 7

The detriment and paradox of modern cancer "cures."

*T*he term "cure" is health wise, contentiously, legally and actually very misunderstood, has overtures of misleading and can leave a disappointed and angry state of mind after the process is finished. Why?

The term "cure" has connotations of presenting an absolute change from bad to good; assuming a physical condition is bad and the cure is good. Let's see. A breast cancer lingered and was removed to prevent further metastasis. The patient recovered minus a breast. Months passed and cancer mutation erupted adjacent to the breast. Medical analysis dictated treatment to eradicate "all" the area cells which left the rib area in a nonusable condition, but was considered cured. The patient recovered minus useable ribs.

Is that a cure? A cure is to bring a bad condition back to normal, not a bad condition to a worse condition.

A series of drugs and surgical treatments were administered for cancer. It resulted in shrunk flesh and bone which left the patient permanently immobilized and depressed, but the cancer was gone for the time. The procedure was considered a successful "cure." A cure is a cure when the patient returns to normalcy, not to being permanently handicapped.

A patient receives chemotherapy treatments for cancer and is "cured" of a local cancer. He is 45 years old and told the chances are it can return in five years which will require more of the same treatments. Each time it gets worse with age.

The side effects of this patient are long term and creates multiple side effects mentally, emotionally, physically and domestically with no chance to change and yet each successful treatment is considered to have cured the cancer at that point.

If people don't get checked for cancer regularly, especially if they live lives exposed to toxins, alcohol, smoking and the continued list of carcinogenic initiators, many of the times initially inflicted cancer metastasizes and its spreading weakens a healthy cure for long life and/or retaining organs or limbs.

If one could only see a ballpark or two filled with conventional cancer "cures," one might be willing to pay more attention to what happens in an era of cancer mutation victims and turn to preventive and/ or wholistic methods for retaining their body parts and peace of mind. Then, when one waits too long for professional care, surgery will probably extend one's life some.

Twenty first century cancer is largely drugged, treated and cut out or off by conventional methods. Our medical institutions and insurance companies work hand in hand to solve and resolve the problems of cancer and yet we have more cancer now than ever costing more than ever and yielding more dismayed medical recipients. This century is also developing better wholistic methods.

Sure, many recipients have fully recovered, too. Why not all of them in this speedily acquiring society with all its advancements? The answer to that is simple and unadulterated. The "society" just isn't promoting or practicing wholistically natural methods physically, psychologically and yes, spiritually too. They are too slow in bending toward natural methods and mistrust the most valuable asset there is in any "cure" which utilizes conscious patience of mind power and its serious application plus endless access of nutritional information of food and supplements along with more wholesome daily activities including sufficient exercise, laughter, pure water and avoiding toxins in many ways to mention a few of the health assets sufficiently available. Where reason to survive normally is desired, people can be trained to use their power of mind effectively.

A cure for anything or anyone is to reduce the symptoms down to zero, not to reduce a person's body parts down to zero through the elimination process of drugs plus surgery "only."

Conventional and wholistic solutions disagree somewhat similar to democrats and republicans. We know they "can" join one another along with world governments in bending and flexing with one another. They are all aware of heading in that direction, but at present, it only appears to be surface talk. The climate change problem is beginning to join more nations in our common causes. In the meantime, we individuals can "choose" our methods for resolving local problems along with cancer and other self-inflicted diseases. We just need to get with it a little more seriously and quicker whether it's through politics "or" goals of longevity.

Understandably, the process of change "is" a growth process where more evidence is needed and broadly helpful especially when problem finding people are objectively focused on and with nonconventional, nonpatterned and nondestructive solutions of disease prevention and its maintenance.

Even as I, your author, unroll these views, suggestions and possibilities, I have to deal with my rather steadfast, set and habitual mannerisms contending I'm right and my way is the only way. I have to bend and flex too because, although belief is the most powerful support within the human system of mind toward any objective, submitting or rendering ideas brought in from unexplored sources or even areas of fantasy and wishful thinking can leave me very mistaken and a subject of hypothetical, misdirected, hypocritical or condemned interrogation. It behooves me to think what I know about health stability may not be conclusive, therefore it becomes time to cross examine my professed contentions so they unfold in a reasonably acceptable manner pertaining to being helpful in nonhindrence methods of dealing with cancer prevention and/or management; that is, in my somewhat limited area of healthcare expertise.

One of the major problems most cancer victims face even without being aware of it, is an inability to fully or many times even partially understand past and present influences contributing to cancer mutation and metastasis formation so they can make personally calculated decisions about preventing or stopping the negative formation.

The result of this lack of knowing renders most victims easy pray or subjects to be dealt with in the only way conventional beliefs understand which is with drugs and/or surgery, generally. We must continually gain more knowledge on this subject.

The paradox of these practices in the conventional approach is where the patient doesn't accept enough responsibility for his or her existence, health or survival. They only respond to the control and direction of the hired professional which, many times, isn't sufficient or appropriate. The more the professional tells the patient what to do, the more chances are of the patient constantly calling that professional for help. That would never work in this time of fast office calls and "no" phone calls accepted. So what happens? The prescribed pills tides the patient over passively until the next visit etc., etc. Very little meaningful progress takes place without more personal attention—or—with the educated knowledge, in this case, of the cancer victim or cancer preventer (someone else accepting responsibility to help). They "can" be a plus or better.

Advancements in health and prevention methods thrive and prosper when and where the individual wholeheartedly accepts responsibility along with help of literature, professionals and internet etc. More is accomplished because the individual is constantly promoting better health day by day with wholistic/natural methods relating with some conventional methods. That's fair play in the health industry.

I never ignore how our conventional medical/ surgery methods have their necessary place in our human and animal health scene. We just need to rationally discern the difference for applying which one to use so we don't become further "victims" of choices where they weren't more consistently related for better and future purposes.

Professional health care directors are many times very limited in their vocal/verbal and application procedures with their patients because of legal worries erupting occasionally due to either so many unforeseen surprises in body or mind response or patient interpretation of procedure or treatment and results. Those actions and results have placed a heavy burden on the meaningful intentions of helping to guide patients with a free spirited approach where the professional doesn't have to be up tight defending himself with every word or movement and consequently, some less affectively guided procedures.

The word "cure" doesn't even want to be mentioned any more because of legal ricochets and annoying implications of supposed wrong doing.

So what happens to the apprehensively dangling patient? Actually, it's what "doesn't" happen to the patient. The conventional professionals have to practice by very strict rules and are not allowed to vary much from them.

Wholistic health and procedures dealing with nature and her vast affiliates are not nearly constricted to complications of making major and very technical changes in the body or mind and can flow with nature. Therefore, the use of the word cure doesn't wholly apply. The affected body condition simply returns to a normal state, whatever normal was originally.

The advantage in a dedicated practice of spiritual, psychological and wholistic cures are where the individual does the greater majority of the knowledgeable application (the work) possibly after receiving professional education and guidance. Some people utilize that personally educated knowledge from books, classes, seminars plus viewing and listening to other patients, doctors and medical and/or wholistic oriented TV programs on health.

The least and best process or method may be a detriment for another. What one believes in and supports, many times, "is" best. Cases do vary.

Chapter 8

The relationship of population expansion to cancer

$\mathcal{T}$he population expansion does have a lot to do with why cancer disease has been so aggressive as the number two national self-inflicted disease.

History reminds us of catastrophic virus diseases which killed hundred of thousands of people without their having protective defense against it. It seems each century has had its share. Most contagious diseases took their course like the black plague and leprosy etc. and eventually disappeared.

Cancer seems like an epidemic. It's so prevalent with all society's classes of people and yet it hasn't been classified as an epidemic even though it has affected so many people.

Heart disease has been the number one killer, but not as spooky as cancer. Nothing really shows with heart disease. Cancer can become very putrid and unpleasant to view just as leprosy was several decades ago.

All this disease business which has spread around so much in recent centuries has to be attributed to some noticeable cause. That's basic. Cause and effect, right?

Centuries ago, there wasn't health threatening words like toxins, plague, smog, contaminate, ozone, BHT, BHA, charred, hydrolyze, additives, pollute and a host of others of which describes conditions and elements of changing the natural to unnatural thereby requiring a need of unnatural human remedies, antidotes, treatments or so called cures.

Prior to the advent of the population increasing in a noticeably fast manner creating crowds everywhere, everything was reasonably natural and hurry wasn't the word for the day's activities. Doctors and hospitals were few and far apart. They only increased when the population increased. That's when the run of the mill diseases became more noticeable. The more people entered the world, the more disease entered too. Cancer was running neck and neck with the other diseases. The twentieth century became the real noticeable increase in the population after a few big wars.

People went wild to expand in everything of families, money, power, food, drink, travel and everything they could get their hands on; including more and new diseases. They followed up with other countries expanding and disease trailed. Along with that disease trailing, cancer was part of it all everywhere. It's been like a free for all with not much regulation. I call it nonprevention methods. They all seemed oblivious to investing time and effort into looking ahead and preparing.

Then came aids. What could be worse than aids and cancer both in the same person. They asked for it. Society waited too long to educate, program and practice preventive and better hygienic habits for better health. Most of it could have been prevented.

Sometime the world of people will be made to realize everything in our earthly environment has a way of working, playing and resolving for our benefit or for our detriment; especially when we allow our planet to be overpopulated.

Sure, growth is healthy and needed for our desired progress, but definitely not gargantuous amounts of extra people. That only adds to more future headaches for everyone because they are being born and saved faster than they can care for themselves. We are getting to the point in this population expansion where it's pretty bad to realize saving new born babies is contributing to a negative producing world population expansion. Very few will even discuss that dilemma.

World regulation of disease isn't efficient enough to handle so many people. It's gotten "out of hand" similar to our climate change, aids and financial chaos.

All of these world and health resolutions, good or bad, flow along with fastly grown overabundances. No one or people can handle it and if they could, they would have too much power that could be leashed out and make slaves out of everyone and use their decrepit bodies to feed the animals or whatever.

Individual control over cancer and other self-inflicted disease, especially a spiritually wholistic belief and approach, is a method for preventing a mass armageddon of desperate and dieing people because of two many too fast!

I, your author, have written two foretelling books called "The Paradox Of Progress Unfolding" book #1 and book #2 that describes possibilities of what "can" happen with this dreaded burden of overpopulation which is more graphically written, but without the disease factors taking their toll. See the list.

More people have entered into this world of mankind presenting a continuous flow of more problems, diminishing fresh water and more complications in the battle of maintaining good health.

When we straighten out our bad habits and adapt to reasonable and more natural methods for improving our world of people, animals, insects, better and lasting water with really caring in mind, the diseases and damaging psychosocialistic nature of mankind will trickle down just like cancer and resolve with new and more meaningful improvements. Let's engage it.

Our world of mankind may be saved after all. It's like they keep saying on TV, "We have a lot of work to do." That means we "all" have to do the work and believe in it for best results. Free loaders only add to the burdens of poor health and rampant population growth that spurns more uncontrolled disease as cancer and other self-inflicted disease.

Free loaders are people who do nothing for something. Generally, the only thing they keep doing is having babies they cannot take care of or expect other people to do the work while they sit! Consequently, those offsprings and lazy daisies don't learn much about health and survival or why cancer suddenly erupts; so that psychobiological consciousness keeps spreading.

The overpopulation adds low class health and low class relationships that, in turn, perpetuates more of the same. Most health clinics and hospitals are burdened and overrun with lower class people and uncontrolled problems because of their upline lack of effective parental guidance in preventive methods of almost everything.

Before the population bursted, rampant and out of control self-inflicted disease wasn't an issue. Now it is and just barely managed. The less it is managed, in "all" respects, the worse it gets. Let us all cool down and broaden our scope for conquering cancer by devising a plan whether it is internationally,

nationally, in our local community or in our own house that will contribute in an effective manner toward reducing the world's population somehow and conquering cancer.

Local gabbing about the growing population actually creating cancer among several different groups and nations etc, will help spread the word where corrections are needed.

Present ignorance of cancer/population relationship is a definite threat to our long term survival and at the rate of mankind's volume growth beside the malignant factors in individuals, we are technically and presently speeding up an eventual extinction of mankind due to so many uncontrolled diseases physically, industrially, socially, psychologically "and" especially procreatively. This is no way to reduce the population.

Staying focused on cancer in this book anyway, there isn't enough money or resources to completely stamp out cancer for a disease of the past at least in this day of age. Societies of the world seem more interested in putting money more into making money for what seems a necessity of power and pleasure than for the survival of mankind.

The only solutions for this snowball or domino effect deterioration at present is for each one of us to realize this approaching dilemma and assume more responsibility in better managing our own individual protection against cancer as seems necessary to mention so much in this book.

Wishing for another more effective way to solve this world wide problem of cancer dominance at present, other than adapting to natural methods, has very little creative substance. We "can" be more creative in surviving than we have been.

Yes, creative methods of eliminating the almost onslaught of cancer, especially in such a time of technological additions and improvements in almost everything, is needed more than ever "because" of the obvious population expansion of which has gotten what we might call out of hand in this time of accelerating progress where control of it all doesn't seem to exist, at least at the present time.

Sure, there are so many issues to be considered in this whole world and every nation is striving and struggling to produce national necessities and power over others through competition, wars and words, to say the least, where chaos is increasing instead of decreasing and no one seems to know how to tone it down. Do you? Do they? Does anyone? Let's contend and maybe even speculate a little!

The people of the world seem to have the impression, from what they have been learning if you will, where study and research for advancing the needs of humans is the solution when they just might be advancing the causes of cancer in the process while creating material and psychobiological toxins of a carcinogenic influence. This indicates the harder they try in the process of improvements, the worse it gets.

Beside understanding cancer and dealing with it through what we might call wiser methods than the "usual," demoting so much progress, expansion and population may suffice as well or better than any common solution; especially in preventing the population expansion. That would be "so" great. Read your author's "Preventing The Doom Of Mankind" concerning that possibility.

Chapter 9

The paramount necessity of making choices concerning cancer

*O*bjective desire of necessity has to be at the helm and agreed by the majority for diverging a society of normal and abnormal people along with other life away from a course of dreaded end. Making decisions of how to do this is philosophically connected in how to deal with cancer.

Philosophy, in this respect of managing disease is centered more on all views except "conventional" religion. The scope, beliefs, traditions and controversial aspects of Bible professing is much too extensive and therefore appropriately limited in any influentially spiritual or wholistic descriptions of text in this book.

Planning ahead, as in almost everything desired, is what will allow one to deal with cancer whether it personally affects the individual or whether it is empathizing, sympathizing with or helping someone else who has been affected. Planning ahead means acquiring different views on the subject, knowing someone who has or had cancer and ask, "What would I do if I became a victim?" The more one says, "I don't know," the more chances there are of making painful, irreconcilable or irreversible errors of judgment in approach. Plan ahead. Don't be sorry later. Extended and innovated efforts are needed.

History has shown there have been too many people who were completely unaware of which route to go with when or if they were confronted with cancer or even any other serious disease. Once again, don't be sorry. Develop some open choices. Think of it as possibilities, not absolutes.

Let's get with it and look at what is real. Let's refrain from allowing others to make us believe their way. Search it out with time necessary in understanding the full value of deciding on four basic options available for dealing with cancer. #1 is the medical and/or surgery method, #2 is the wholistic manner, #3 is the conventionally religious manner and #4 is the use of spiritual psychology (mind power within. See my book "Understanding The Science Of Creative Mind"). A combination of any of them can also be helpful as long as one doesn't contradict the other. If that happens, the door is open for more insight to reduce confusion or bewilderment.

Make a decision whether the medical doctor, the shrink, the minister, the belief of the individual, the wholistic practitioner or a divine source is running the show of cancer management. Utilizing all of them at the same time may be a detriment to the cause. These decisions are paramount in either moving forward enriching the process of defeating cancer or losing the battle depending on the strength of mind that may or may not fully support the cause. If these goals are not established and exercised thoroughly, chances of conquering cancer completely are not quite as favorable. The natural way requires personal attention from the preventer, the victim or anyone else who helps guide the individual.

Decisions must never be haphazardly made. They must be a result of rationally developed beliefs based on evidence revealed and coupled with enough experiences which help guide the way toward initiating decisions. One must feel confident in making these decisions. The data and experiences all add toward meaningful accomplishments from those decisions.

Decisions must be made first. Then a determined and confident choice can be directed. Those who depend on medicine and/or surgery usually do not assume responsibility for their "whole" lives and are at the mercy of conventional methods.

Cancer is a disease that "picks" on vulnerable immunity. We can be born with genetic cancer tendency from parents of whom had the same tendencies. It's not "just" a passing down of the genes as though they were like a box of marbles that remains the same as they were; to say nothing about them other than, "That's the way they were." They were that way because of their parent's habits and culture. That changes every time another generation of new and different people procreate. Cancer genetic tendencies can be changed to the point of stopping the genetic growth of cancer by planning, initiating believing and steadily practicing what was efficiently planned. This is referred to as profound programming which is very similar to that of praying except it is conducted by the self "to" the self. It works! Anyone can do it by being serious about it.

Sometimes the inherited vulnerabilities causing cancer remain the same depending on cultural habits, good or bad diets, good or bad water or air, good exercise or none, exposure to anything contaminating, good or poor social or hygienic exposure and the usual long list of contributors to vulnerability. Cancer itself can become the victim and fade away with serious wholistic practice and especially its belief in it.

Our minds are the most powerful assistance we have in changing anything within ourselves. Most people go through life wasting that potential. Anyone who has achieved confidence in any particular area has been using that power. The same can by done with cancer. Straighten out the act and the cancer straightens out. Continue with the negative belief where one cannot buck genetics and one may experience much more difficulty in bucking cancer.

New methods of spiritual transformation (the power of belief within) is slowly happening world wide. I wrote a book a while back called "Evaluating Outdated Beliefs." It explains this transforming new way of thinking, believing and approach toward achieving a more confident manner of life here on planet Earth. Other than that, there are many worth while approaches in preventing cancer or whipping it. Let us allow ourselves to practice them whether we are preventing cancer, whether we currently have it, whether we are ridding ourselves of it or whether we are not experiencing it at all. The knowledge is priceless. Warning, the book mentioned about "exposing" outdated beliefs is very controversial.

Remember that famous saying, "What goes around, comes around?" The influential factors causing cancer are circulating around more profoundly than ever. Don't let that programming affect your choices concerning your health maintenance. The subconscious mind absorbs it and is highly influential in triggering cancer mutation. Choose your best route. Avoid those factors and program eliminating cancer mutation. This pertains to the self as well as helping someone else.

Believing in what we say and do one hundred percent along with other wholistic practices mentioned periodically and other books I have written gets positive results. I practice what I preach and I'm shooting for a very long and youthful life. It will be described in my new books accordingly.

If there was ever a class needed in school or elsewhere, one on the psychology, science, consciousness and even art of developing the ability of making choices could surely be helpful. Reading literature on the subject can be insightful and add toward the subject's guidance, but the exchanges of making decisions in a specialized manner through group dynamics would certainly stimulate the process. Any kind of group would be helpful as long as it is done deliberately to meet the goals of making decisions. Yes, this definitely adds toward controlling cancer tendency and its management. Choices come first.

This book is on cancer, but the beliefs, practices and approaches are similar to other illnesses and problems; everything being so relative, that is.

Whatever source concocted the human brain along with the body arrived at it in a super magnificent manner with its amazing abilities to figure, heal, react, move and make flexible changes "all" through life. We must not let that priceless ability go to waste especially when their may be a time of great need. Preventing gross disease before it ignights is one of those times. Look how people weeped "after" they discovered their cancer. Most people have suffered the effects of cancer and the treatments of it when it could have been averted. All that would have been needed would have been a choice to prevent cancer and the odds would have been in favor of that destiny. Odds are all we have to work with since their are so many contributing factors toward acquiring self-inflicted disease. There are no absolute possibilities; only odds of them.

Moving ahead having acquired cancer, the choice abilities are still almost miraculously available. That power is still there. That power to choose or change in the middle of the dilemma can mean more power to gather more knowledge for gaining more confidence which allows more support for a chosen route that will either whip the cancer problem completely—or—maybe only for a bit. Maybe the "choice" was only an overriding piece of advice from a firmly set view which was only concerned with supporting that set view and not particularly caring to expand with new and/or future innovation and successes.

Business corporations are merging together left and right with effective, sincere and successful ventures for the benefit of surviving better in joining with new ideas for stronger financial balance and for better service to the community etc. It's nothing new. Why can't the healthcare industry do something similar? If the cancer cells knew that was happening, they would probably start running knowing the people made choices that would contribute toward chasing them away.

Choosing a route to go with cancer is breaking the barrier that prevents actualizing one's direction.

Then one acquires that power of confidence to move forward with whatever the choice is.

This chapter is pointing out the necessity and power within pertaining to gathering reason for making choices. This time it's a serious matter of pooling one's history of either constantly going along with what others say or seeking out solutions to everything confronted. Which is it? That gathered history may just tell one which direction one may end with the subject of cancer.

The tendency for the average person in promoting better health for long life and preventing illness is just to let it happen without much thought on the subject. That means very little effort is engaged in making decisions for initiating "any" kind of health program for preventing illness such as cancer in this case. It's no wonder there is so much of it feeding the societies of unsuspecting people who appropriate time for other necessities of which have nothing to do with staying healthy and living a stronger, stable and disease free existence.

The average person waits too long to gain knowledge for preventing ill health and what happens? Cancer creeps in.

Making no choice is making "a" choice to do nothing. Think about it. Changing one's ways may seem somewhat awkward, but doing it with insight for a better future is well worth it.

Placing emphasis on making decisions on prevention matters, treatments and lifestyle is "the" most important issue first.

Chapter 10

Further understanding how cancer forms

$\mathcal{W}$e know there are several factors contributing to cancer mutation. Cancer is also predisposed to infection. There are doctors outside the borders of the U.S. who believe the combination of certain body cell mutation and low stage infection enhance one another; therefore may be referred to as cancer infestation and are treated with potent doses of supplements, herbs, specialty substances as Laetrile and others with what appears to have gotten and is still getting good results.

Common knowledge of disease cell breakdown professes weak or weakened body cells from genetic or other factors in specific areas where any type infection lingers tend to increase the odds of cancer mutation whether acutely or chronically initiated under the continued adverse exposure to health.

Remission doesn't mean massive cells have been "killed" as in conventional methods. It means there is a transmutation of affected cells relaxing and healing while slowly returning to normal. The affected area may remain swollen, but is once again healthy with continued individual discipline exercised.

There is no absolute rule of thumb covering cancer from the beginning forward. That means one must remember every cancer case is a little different and still others a lot different. So far, these scripts have only generalized on cancer, its origin, development and possible approaches in its maintenance to end it with controlled continuity where discipline is utilized.

Cancer is a self-inflicted nuisance thriving in or on spots and spreads outward until it devours the whole person if left unchecked. If checked early enough, it can be eliminated as is mentioned throughout this book.

Cancer, like anything else living, depends on consuming to fulfill its appetite, generally speaking. If it is denied its opportunity to thrive, it withers away. That means if the nutrients for its survival are either not available or in another case denied by the disciplined individual, its cancerous effects or progress won't form according to all that is wholistically deducted along with proven cases. Technically, the cancer effects will be referred to as less active in a productive manner and is in a process of remission.

The question is always what constitutes it permanently inactive. The forces of evil, negativity, dominancy and the like will probably always prevail waiting for the easy opportunities to pounce on. Cancer somehow knows when and where the vulnerable places are to devour and begins its exploitation. What stops the triggering cancer mutation in its tracks? It is either a healing and strong immune system which is almost the same as preventing it from a beginning mutation, an act of normal T cells warding off cell mutation or a combination of both; certainly not a run down or genetically weak system of mind and body cells. Those must be built up.

We all have strong "and" weak tendencies of some nature. Most of us have little awareness of that fact and furthermore do very little, if anything to sway, alter or change that state of being. When one is told a serious disease like cancer has formed, that person panics and wants it stopped pronto and not only is a victim of self-inflicted disease, for the most part, but also allows being a victim of quick fix methods initiating surgery, burning or doping the natural human system reducing natural necessities of life.

Many times these victimized people are so terrorized by the fear inflicted suggestions of health failure heading toward unknown and advancing deterioration and sickness, they don't take time to learn and practice eliminating cause tendencies propagating the disease. Then, with their fear oriented and justified decisions, they end up many times with either a worse condition from toxic drug contamination, hospital death from errors made or finally left without an organ or more or a limb or more and no guarantee of permanent cure many times because the patient resumes previous habits which caused the mutation in the first place without consciousness of it.

A typical mind set belief seems to be for one to somehow eliminate or even, as is said, eradicate the cancer cells for a complete cure. That may apply where an immediate threat to life is concerned, but only in that case which really needs more rational evaluation. There is a possibility a patient of that vulnerability may not survive the medical, surgical or both approach and procedure.

There are great advantages for one to keep in mind: Cancer growth is not necessarily an endless progress of illness and everlasting deterioration. It only occurs, as is pointed out in different manners in this book, when the source of its propagation is continually distributed or "fed" into the human system. Destroying cancer cells along with the healthy cells through surgical application etc. is conventionally practiced and of course, fairly respected even by me, your author because of it's laboriously researched contributions toward efforts in gaining meaningful headway on disease control of which we essentially need. However, there are also other meaningfully researched views adding to that control.

Time and experience is continually adding to and supporting evidence revealing resistance to cancer cell residence which means all the body's cells remain healthy and strong until such a time when strong genetical influence, age, toxin exposure factors or all of them weigh heavily on the human system and reduces their natural strength in specific areas.

Where and when maintenance of good health throughout life continues through natural methods, the odds favor very little tendency for carcinogenical mutation. If the body's T cells are functioning normally as the design of life, all the cells will remain healthy and not break down when exposed to temporary "or" terminal illnesses; even further time consuming illnesses.

The option to T cell protection, if not functioning properly, is for the acquired knowledge of mankind to tap the files of the individual for his or her weakness influences that could or did contribute to cell deterioration. When that or those factors are gathered, action must be supported in bringing those weaknesses up to par through all these natural and wholistic mannerisms mentioned in this and possibly other books on building our inefficient immune system or diligently supporting, improving and appreciating the value of our already strong immune system.

If cancer has formed, being overly concerned about dealing with and treating the affected cancer cells may not be largely or nearly as beneficial as concentrating more on firmly maintaining the normal and healthy cells or building up the struggling cells which have not yet been carcinogenically affected. Remaining or developing cellular strength automatically prevents or resolves cancer cell action. The reenergized immune system has a natural way of living with discouraged cancer cells of which also resolve in a natural manner especially when the original and natural immune system is restored with continuous support.

Many medically trained doctors say to not worry about your immune system and shrug it off as a too complicated and time consuming effort for them. Along with that, most insurance companies won't pay for examinations or any extended treatments concerning this negative condition which indicates the healthcare system lacks wholistic support for the benefit of the patient preventing disease (cancer in this case). Most conventional doctors don't allow time to educate patients unfortunately. Books of this nature can be helpful if patients are willing to read them.

The doctors and insurance companies are very hesitant in supporting any natural method of approach because it shakes their boat! They want the income to stay the same without changes requiring more effort and less money. Presently and hopefully just for now, this is their mindset and the only way it will change is for people to start squawking and raising their consciousness.

That view on doctors and insurance companies may seem what anyone can refer to as cynical or a mistaken opinion, so I suggest the reader check it out. If enough of you do, what I am saying along with your efforts, natural methods may come into play and serve "all" of whom are concerned.

Notifying their government representatives to initiate legislature would adopt "both" prescription drugs "and" wholistic remedies. Health progress would then accelerate with combined efforts of everyone involved. Both sides must join.

Sure, money is at the bottom of it all. Everyone knows that by now. The positive view is insurance companies would profit with less claims, lobbyists would save money, pharmaceutical companies could adjust their overall prices on drugs and supplements etc. to sustain that business industry, the doctors and hospitals could be relieved of overburdening debt and legal problems plus the people would maintain better health and overall happiness. It "can" happen. Let us join in this effort, not fight one another.

The education needed for cancer patients or people who desire to prevent cancer must supersede any ignorance in health care availability. The public has to know more about cancer function and the common sense required for making individual choices of one's lifestyle in preventing and/or managing any development of cancer. We all deserve to manage our lives better by accepting this responsibility.

The health care officials are beginning to stage more seminars on these subjects. Let's seek them out and wherever else for this life saving knowledge beside this book and others available.

Chapter 11

Further "understanding" of preventing cancer

$\mathcal{P}$reventing cancer growth is about the same as what is referred to as reversing it. When one applies methods in preventing cancer, the progress of the cancer breaks down. The body condition remains about the same. When one acquires a cancer growth and reverses it, as they say, the growth slows down and stops. The disfiguration will look and remain about the same as time passes, but the mutation process cannot continue when weakened vulnerability is no longer nourished, supported or programmed due to disciplined changes made by the individual whether alone or with help.

Any growth on the human or animal species of living beings has a specific and reactionary reason for its existence. It didn't just appear for no reason. The statement has been heard many times, "We doctors don't know why." Lack of training? Could be. Not knowing why releases their responsibility of health commitments, approaches and resolutions. There "are" reasons why anything grows in the body. We just need to be a little more creative, realistic and comprehensive in dealing with them.

A nonmalignant growth is usually considered a common tumor and only a nuisance. There are certain factors that sprouted up through the protoplasmic and biological process that initiated the tumor. That tumor is generally considered a mass of flesh, edema, bone or other basic body substance and viewed or treated similarly to that of a hernia. Like a hernia, more often than not, the common tumor isn't a serious concern unless there is an unusual change in appearance, persistent pain, fever or nausea etc. Care must be applied in discerning the difference between the terms of common tumors and potentially adverse cell change. A tumor does spread and can become quite large, but is usually in one lump area. Cancer, by contrast, metastasises (travels) extensively throughout the bloodstream if not retarded or brought to a stop. Check out all these contentions as I am not a doctor.

There have been and presently are circles of debate as to an exact deduction of whether a tumor is common and nonthreatening relative to its possibility of being a family member of very threatening cancer growth. Time will tell.

A common tumor may be benign in its spreading effect, but remember, body condition may be the reason it "is" benign. The body condition always has the potential to change and sometimes quite rapidly where one is exposed to many sometimes sudden environmental, emotional, physical or social influences; maybe all of them. Do not look, once again, for a rule of thumb for everything. They change too. Deal constantly with new and possible differences in time, circumstances and situations. Achieving, gaining or maintaining top health integrity by efficient methods is totally necessary. Natural methods do that. Just be serious with them.

Cancer, with its individual growth and environmental infestation, has fairly clear indications of being relatively connected with all the influential factors mentioned and is also growing with the population expansion. We "must" slow it down!

Medical science can run the rat race of attempting to retain its pursuit of offsetting, curing or even complicating the plight of cases of cancer around the world, but they are not equipped to handle them all nor can all the people pay for it. So what happens or what "is" happening? Read on.

Our inner health and our environment world wide has historically existed as two completely different entities. Now they are more swiftly integrating as functional partners having some conflicts and attempting to fix them. Hah, it is that creeping closeness of massive people exposed and interrelating with environmental junk in almost all respects that perpetuates all our influences upon one another. Cancer is a subject of an environmentally enclosed factors infestation.

Now there may be too many people and complications with being close and dependent concerning our inner health and our environment. A whole nation is attempting to "fix" the problem of cancer; some doing it and some lousing it up by not dealing with the "factors" causing it.

Dealing with the reality we all must face requires our best possible working solution which is to manage ourselves better in a wholistic manner; one that requires us to accept more responsibility in caring and offsetting influential ills by doing it ourselves "with" professional guidance.

More specifics are ahead. Hang in there.

Chapter 12

Adopting new ideas for eliminating rockset deception will help in dealing with cancer along with present knowledge

All we have is what we have at present. We will have immensely more if and when we allow ourselves to remain open and absorb more controversial and provable methods. We "can" extend our lives out long enough to reap the harvest of all that has been learned for more meaningful use.

Learning how to effectively adapt in understanding cancer requires interest in the subject hopefully from a distance and not from a victim's viewpoint. Without sincere interest, a person won't "seek

out" more necessary data for forming efficient analysis allowing that understanding. Next, learning how cancer effects some people and not others is priceless for cross examining and eliminating gobbledy gook opinions based on speculation and/ or sheer belief. Cancer has been referred to as the complicated disease. That's why most of the victims are like putty in the hands of unscrupulous "healers" and fine tuned professionals who are primarily money oriented and care more about the money than the patient's condition. This definitely has to change.

Certified professionals are necessary for help and sometimes totally dependent on by patients who lack self-sufficiency and the capability to sustain health and life through their own powers of pursuance. Let us choose the right ones.

Sure, cancer is a little too complicated for most people to successfully deal with since a rule of thumb doesn't always apply to everyone. However, since cancer strikes so many people like heart disease, becoming more conscious of what really "has" happened with cancer victims can be steps and reasons to stave off cancer wherever possible. That doesn't mean one should "worry" or fret over it. It just means to be aware there is a threat lingering over everyone and as any other threat, we "can" adopt a defense line type of attitude to offset the odds.

There is too much deceptive consciousness where getting cancer means one will die from it. That state of continuous consciousness "can" perpetuate a belief of death being inevitable because of it. Effective belief, selected choices and practicing them daily is what supports the creative actions of mind and produces its reality within as a program, so watch it! That program may unfold as a negative reality of forming cancer mutation if pondered on in a worrisome and fearful manner similar to what happens when suddenly faced with a ground animal, a shark in the ocean or a hostile human. If they sense one's uncontrolled fear, the odds are they will attack much more than if one remains cool, calm and collected.

There "is" thought, belief, theory and research pending where the possibility of our body cells, including the cells carcinogenically effected, can live and function by guided intelligence, not particularly instinct or tendency. That theory makes sense to me. I believe our minds control and direct our whole entity. I call it headquarters (our brain). Whatever we think, from our inherited tendencies or newly programmed influence, is what forms our entity of mind.

We can allow ourselves to genetically and inherently exist with little or no developed control over our psycho and biological entity or we can choose to and develop that control depending on how we have allowed ourselves to exercise the privilege of making choices. That privilege of choice is delved into in my other books covering a very sensitive subject where most people are extremely resistant to relinquishing "any" rock hard, programmed and security oriented contentions. Searching them out will be rewarding.

How sad it is to see how massive amounts of people are so limitedly contained under the deceptive control of conventional methods when there "are" other and many times more beneficial methods which can enhance self-control as compared to being controlled by others.

This book on cancer is one of which is centered on the obvious subject along with emphasis on being self-sufficient while remaining aware of available help from outside the self.

My book on spiritual transformation ahead in time is a little controversial, but it will reveal the self-sufficient abilities one has even when one doesn't realize it. It may influence the world of concept to a point of being more capable than ever of solving and resolving the seemingly inescapable woes and ways of what mankind has created in the overall health of mind, body and environmental disposition. The future minded may embrace it. The past minded may disregard it. It's overdue to be viewed. I still remain humble in my views where all is not written or intended as absolute in contention, but with knowledge that destiny also has its wavers in time and we will, hopefully, always render our choices to do the same.

Presently, we will stick to the woes, ways, hindrances and elimination of cancer birth and our battles against it.

Yes, cancer is definitely a battle for so many affected and afflicted; mostly from not knowing its cellular function, not gaining knowledge of it's capabilities, not practicing many manners of prevention and finally due to ignoring them, not having periodical checkups which can indicate to "change one's ways."

There is a great factor in cancer awareness, prevention and control. It is that of luck. Luck really has no bases to it. No skill can be attributed to it. No rhyme or reason will support or justify it, but it is still there. Sure, luck always lingers and can be considered very spiritual. Many people believe luck will prevail for best benefits if they keep praying. True, luck is something that means favorable results can unfold, but generally, what triggers it or allows it is only interpretable by the individual based on what is in that individual's mind.

Many religious circles claim the belief of luck is a divine spirit at work which appears to me as a metaphorical contradiction of spirit. To each his own. Let's keep it open for thought.

I say we can fill and exercise our own unique belief of luck with inner spiritual support of many natures already widely nurtured. They bring the mathematics of odds favorably to our side. It "does" require individual effort though. Anything expected without effort is only wishful thinking. Sorry, wishful thinking only rates as zero on a list of anything accomplishable. At least we give odds a fair chance of being realistically achievable by working with and nurturing them. Being better at "anything" requires going further with its progress.

Everything meaningfully nurtured "allows" healthier, stronger and more normal development when given a constantly supported chance.

Remember, cancer is not a mysterious or magical disease unknown to mankind. It's been hindering the natures of mankind for probably longer than presently known. The result of that descended history tells us we know it doesn't "just" happen. Cancer has had, in every case from all logical analysis, a definite reason for its cell transformation even though it's not always "clearly" understandable what initially incubates it.

Even without clear knowledge of its origin, we are getting more proefficient at managing cancer with progressively improving equipment for examining and testing thanks mostly to conventional methods. The doctors, hospitals, cancer institutions, researchers and nurses etc. all deserve due credit for their contributing efforts even though this author is a bit biased to the natural and wholistic methods for managing unhealthy conditions of living beings.

The following are a few guidelines which can be very helpful in being more responsible for preventing self-inflicted disease such as cancer and other ills propagated by unhealthy, genetical and environmental influences:

Guideline 1. Be aware, cancer formation starts with genetic influence of its previous life style and immune system disorders. If possible, check out those inherited and present tendencies for analyzing and planning preventive methods. Otherwise analyze the same of the self and proceed appropriately with the preventive methods according to known strengths and weaknesses.

Guideline 2. Cancer growth is susceptible to forming when one has been and/or is exposed to toxic material from auto, home, industrial liquids and gases and other chemical substances plus undue stress caused by continuous social, business, family or political etc. pressure and, of course, the very unhealthy junk food such as anything fried, dried, overcooked, burnt, brittle, shriveled, preserved, unnatural, poorly fed, cheaply produced, super finely ground, artificial, processed or generally boxed. Junk food reduces certain system elasticity and strength (genetic or otherwise) thereby encouraging cancer mutation from the carcinogenic junk food processing.

Guideline 3. Avoid surgery and drugs etc. wherever possible. If the body's cells are genetically predisposed to carcinogenic action when the treatment penetrates the flesh, cancer cells can metastasize further. That could be the beginning of its silently sprouting growth within especially when one's immune system has lessened in its strength as usually does when one gets into their later years. Most people are unaware of this happening day to day, year to year. Catch the mutation early and it can be halted without penetrating methods. Even in that eventuality, serious cancer cell starvation works. Starving the cancer, that is.

Surgery may be necessary in circumstances requiring emergency service or when a reasonable decision is made for correcting a physical deformity and a few other save a life situations where surgery appears to be the "last" resort. Otherwise, there are many other options and they "must" be examined for retaining natural health and physical disposition that contributes toward one living a much longer and natural life.

Any kind of drugs, prescription or hallucinatory, which are not considered food or natural substance are undoubtedly not naturally digestible and must be personally as well as professionally scrutinized for application into the human or animal system. Most of them serve temporary relief of some nature, but for long term recipients, toxic formation gathers and the patient, in so many cases, becomes a deteriorating subject of chemical manipulation or—fiest.

The possibility of those contentions may not "always" apply, though, so using broad discretion in decisions for choosing health improvement methods is better not denied. Using limited or sheer narrow minded discretion may not suffice in improving the immune system for resisting disease. Learn.

Our immune system (cells that resist disease) must be sufficiently maintained. When it is, it automatically unleashes changes that eliminates cancer inflicted attraction. Many times, under stressful and inadequate nutrition etc., our cells become confused as to which ones to reside with. They wonder off and become victims of other deteriorating cells. Prevent that occurrence by becoming disciplinary serious about building a better immune system through these wholistic methods, approaches, practices and attitudes. Make them a way of life. They will serve well. Generally speaking and for the most part, cancer does not occur when the immune system is functioning at its best with the exception of isolated cases.

Hormone treatment may enhance cancer mutation. It's better to refrain from its use. Hormonal balance is an important factor in maintaining a cancer resisting immune system. It can carry cancer cells to other areas of the body. Be aware and question the administrator thoroughly.

Guideline 4. The following is what we need to and need not to eat or drink for preventing and/ or managing cancer: Caution, though, commercial claims of what is organic may be deceiving. Animal fertilizer for plants include the chemicals they treat the animals with and is in the food they feed them. Be sure to check the purity of so called organic food.

Eat variations of fruit. Better ones for cancer prevention or management are red grapes, most berries, pomegranate, cherries and the edible seeds of grapes and apricots. Chew them well for better digestion. Better vegetables for the same cause are cabbage, leafy greens, three colored bell peppers, asparagus, broccoli, mushrooms, onions and brussel sprouts to name a few. Veggies are better cooked less than more. Fruit and veggy juices are also good, but better when sipped. It allows saliva to mix with the juice for better digestion. Everything treated meaningfully favors one's condition. Diet in cancer prevention or management requires continuously serious discipline. Being more creative is a plus to the cause.

Herbs are always a plus in anyone's diet, especially for prevention purposes and cancer management. Cleanse, refresh, purify and preserve body cells for improving the immune system with mistletoe, chaparell, echinacea, kelp, morender, parthenium, red clover, goldenseal, alfalfa, beepollen, burdock and/or elderberry. Use kava kava to relax and sleep. Gotu kola helps dispose unwanted cells.

Raw nuts and seeds are good energy food for the immune system and adds toward preventing and eliminating cancer infected cells; especially raw almonds, walnuts and apricot seeds. Also, brown rice is a must along with other "whole" grain food that serves the same purposes.

Necessary vitamin supplements increase immunity and adds toward decreasing cancer potentiality. When the immune system is strong, the body's flesh, bone and blood are poor places for cancer production to grow. If it had started, it could shrink in its attempts. That's where the term remission is fitting.

Multiple vitamin supplements play a big role in conquering and controlling cancer as well as preventing it. Don't let it slip by.

The use of vitamin supplements, for best results, must be studied and constantly practiced because the body is subjective to change. Thereby, the supplements must change too. Not enough may not help. Too much may cause contamination. That's why most supplement companies sell well balanced capsules or liquids for average health. Proper amino acids are also a must for cancer situations. However, qualified guidance is highly recommended for determining which ones and how much to use. Don't guess with amino acids.

Cancer usually requires the use of blood tests or kinisiology for determining best results with supplements. An average priced multivitamin may suffice in practice for a person of average health in the prevention of any self-inflicted disease. Better protection against those types of diseases may require analyzing health situations using more and specific supplements of specialized nature. Check with specialty professionals in nutritional guidance. They must know one's condition.

Cancer patients have had good results with the following supplements and special remedies which means it will add toward the cause of preventing and eliminating cancer when utilized in appropriately accepted manners. It is always better to consult with an authorized health care professional as well as being responsible for the self. The following is food, herbs and vitamins etc. for those purposes:

1. Wheat germ oil. Use as directed if one can digest oil.
2. Horseradish. Use plenty, but don't overdo.
3. Use potassium sufficiently supplied in potent multicaps or as directed by a professional in cancer care.

4. Distilled water. Use half of daily filtered water.

5. Brewers yeast in bulk, capsule or liquid. Use as directed.

6. Selenium. Use in various forms as directed.

7. Green tea. Sip slowly. Do not drink fast. Add nothing to it.

8. Vit. D. Use at least 400 mg., more if professionally guided.

9. Laetrile and/or special formulas of it, being controversial, "has" had good results through many health care directors especially in Mexico.

10. Enzymes for more complete digestion. Get analyzed for this.

11. Avocados. Especially Haas from California.

12. Wild berries picked and sold in retail markets.

13. Use only top grade fish (from the wild) for cancer care.

14. Olive oil helps prevent carcinogenic action in fried food.

15. Antioxidant supplements as grape seed extract etc.

16. Vit. C. It burns up fast. Use plenty. Follow directions.

17. Red grapes in any form are well known for preventing and treating cancer growth. Also, acai berry softgells are great.

18. Use hydrochloric acid for preventing stomach cancer or its advancement. It prevents or controls putrifaction and fermentation in the digestive track. Good remedy.

19. Use lactic acid and whey for cancer preferably issued by a health care professional.

20. Garlic is a good prevention food for many ills.

21. Phyto nutrients (greens and fruit) can prevent cells from reaching a carcinogenic stage.

Guideline 5. The following is what not to do or use and if adhered to can add toward preventing and/ or eliminating cancer:

1. Bad diet, smoking and heredity are big factors favoring cancer mutation especially in certain African and mid eastern nations. Cancer mutation is the second leading health threat in the U.S. Check it out early.

2. Chemical exposure (toxins) in any form is a dominant influence in acquiring cancer. Be aware. Check them out.

3. Cancer melanoma from sun exposure affects sensitive white skin and people with low resistance as one ages and can metastasize (spread) to other organs. Watch exposure.

4. Too much vitamin A can be toxic. 20,000 units per day may suffice. Chronic cases may need more, but only with knowlegible guidance.

5. Avoid salt, sugar and/or smoked meats. They can cause carcinogenic action (sparks cancer).

6. Avoid anything hydrogenated, homogenized, hydrolyzed and/or preserved (mostly prepared food). Read ingredients.

7. Avoid eating animals treated with hormones, antibiotics or fed with insecticide sprayed grains. Better to buy "all natural" meat and poultry. Also, to beat cancer, use much less meat products. Too much protein of any kind attracts cancer cell growth especially with those who are not physically active. If possible, do without it until well.

8. Only buy fish raised in their natural habitat. Farm raised are fed with unusual food which affects their health stability and consequently ours too. Their process is improving.

9. Avoid smoking and alcoholic drinking. They contribute to mouth, esophagus and liver cancer among other illnesses.

10. Go easy on egg yokes, liver and butter. Although they are loaded with nutrients, they also contribute toward breast, colon and other organ cancer by virtue of their protein and fat. Some cannot handle them especially nonexercisers.

11. Refrain from drinking wine with sulfites (conditioner/preservative) which most do have. It's stated on the bottle.

12. Chocolate has certain values, but is also highly allergenic and comes from an undigestible bean; therefore becomes a detriment toward preventing cancer.

13. Many people cannot digest and assimilate oil of any kind properly in the human system and it hinders normal cells in specific areas. It can trigger carcinoma in weak cells.

14. Avoid fried food. Most frying oil has a low boiling point. When higher temperature is gained, the oil becomes carcinogenic which is burned to the point of serving as a catalyst for causing cancer. The fried food is a cancer maker and causes havoc in the digestive system to say nothing about how fattening it may be to so many people who have little resistance to it.

15. Avoid eating animal food that has been setting in room temperature for hours. It will sit much

longer in the intestines attempting to digest in a much hotter environment and becomes putrified; hence extremely unhealthy and can contribute to cancer in someone's body who is more susceptible to developing it because of bad health habits.

16. Be conscious of infections, festering and lingering infestations for a longer period of time than normal healing time. It could be a low lying cell deterioration which sometimes is referred to as precancerous. Internal infections, particularly in the urinary track area where sediment gathers for long periods of time can breed cancer in this environment without one knowing. Get checked as often as possible. This is one of the main contributing factors toward prostate and/or bladder cancer beside age and some genetic influence. Get rid of infection! It "can" lead to cancer.

17. All the health care authorities agree smoking, specifically, adds toward degenerative

diseases as cancer etc. and shortens life. One must learn, if not yet done, to believe this is one of the real realities of life. Be aware!

18. Learn, understand and have your immune system analyzed for possible alternatives. It may save going through a miserable health problem (in this case, cancer) which could be prevented or curtailed. Do not ignore it.

19. Big city and/or industrial emission exposure for lengthily periods of time is conducive toward body cell deterioration that enhances cancer growth. Give it some thought.

20. Once again, infection materializes in many different manners. It can occur in the body's tissue, in the emotional and mental psyche, in strong influence from family, friends, employment situations and from one's environmental exposure or pressure. In turn, any of those can be an infectious program to the subconscious mind in many ways that "sours" the human system and inadvertently

prepares body cell vulnerability which can lead to cancer or other self-inflicted disease. Remember, no one else actually "did it." The self did it. Accept that responsibility. Do not allow self-destruction and don't let others contribute to it.

Finally, we have worked our way up to what really controls all our actions and reactions beside that of which is physically and materially "dumped" on us without having control over it. Our minds are programmed to perform the way they will #1 inherently from birth, #2 from family influence, #3 from a particular institution, #4 from teachers or from that point forward a series of other dominating influences of which almost everyone either dodges or absorbs in some manner or other. It's all learned. There is no escape. No wonder cancer is called the complicated disease. We were given billions of cells for managing our bodies, but there may be close to that many influences tending to reshape the originally inherited purity of body and mind cells which twists and turns one's perception and perspective from one influence to another. How does one find time to prepare or in this case, program what is necessary for at least offsetting any infiltrating disease or illness? Let's see.

When we are little and young, we don't know how, right? So it may not be a lack of knowledge we carry with us through life causing cancer or anything else. It may be too much clutter of the mind including the highly influential clutter of preparing the very young to fear life and death and feel falsely insecure with many confusing idealistic rules and requirements making one feel guilty and scared to live for fear of what may happen after life is over. Look in to that!

True, this "subject" can get a bit out of hand and that is what can be happening when one is afflicted with a specific, what I call, self-inflicted disease. They get "out of hand" with too much inside and outside the body influence. It doesn't get a "bit" confusing. It can get overwhelmingly confusing without our knowing it and then what happens? The massively conglomerated institutions and medical physicians gain control over disease and illness believing they are philosophically helping societies of people with their experience and study oriented efforts to control disease and illness when they, so many times, make endless mistakes which render patients as victims of the system while they make billions of dollars in the process. Sure, they help as mentioned, but they won't talk about the many failed cases of "practicing" the system.

Wholistic health is the practice and belief of being natural and treating or being treated in a natural way. True, it is difficult to practice "everything" in a natural manner, but we are working at it. After all, the world's people have become so unnatural for such a long time, it will take a while for everyone to understand and agree natural procedures in the overall picture may be a better course of health existence for humanity and now animals too. Let's view some mind preparations:

Praying and programming are similar. They are just different sources to direct them toward or with. One must utilize this miracle type power to offset the debilitating and disproportional effects of cancer or any other threatening self-inflicted disease.

Preventing cancer and eliminating cancer has close similarities. Just before it begins to mutate, the causes are similar to what propels it. When one acquires knowledge as to the cause, whether it has been lingering prior to its mutation or in the maturing process, programming or praying with one's ability to visualize a plan and approach stating it daily will have a definite effect in reducing the speed of the mutation with time. This must be accompanied daily with as many natural remedies mentioned as possible.

Don't ask how long it will take. That would be like asking God how long will it take. This is all a matter of dealing with nature and sometimes (if you will) she takes her sweet time.

Programming and nature work hand in hand very effectively; especially when one supports that belief (just like any other faith).

What efforts one puts forth will be equal to the efforts mother nature puts forth. That's how long it takes. Results will be noticed with constant belief, confidence in self-direction, unending determination and patience. When this is accomplished, a whole new world of self-confidence unfolds where, "I can do anything within." This belief and practice becomes a way of life.

Plan a vocal program which is spoken allowed every day believing 100% in the program. Support that programmed belief of "you" doing it and "you" will realize that power you were born with. It just needs to be nourished, stimulated and practiced.

Gain confidence in the progress of your program. The more confidence one gains in the process, the more one becomes aware of it doing the job. When the time comes for an exame, the wonder of belief and programming/praying is something to look forward to and back on. Program eliminating cancer. It pays.

Prostate cancer info:

The following are personal encounters with cancer that I, your author experienced as the years rolled by: Awhile back when I was in my late thirties, I was making many trips to the bathroom during the day. A few years later, this condition eased its way into the night and disturbed by sleep getting up too much. During that time, I wasn't watching my health habits too well having broken up with my wife after my kids left home. I wasn't feeling too well concerning my emotional stability and where my insecure, frightened and somewhat muzzled life was going.

My doctor informed me I had BPH (benign prostatic hyperplasia), which is said to be swollen prostate and recommended surgery (among other doctors after that) to reduce the swelling. I disagreed that surgery wasn't the solution. They all tried fear tactics to convince me surgery was needed. That was the end of them. Time passed again and I began noticing a worsening of the condition. Another urologist detected infection in the prostate. I didn't like it, but responded to antibiotics. It helped for awhile, but persistently repeated its infections.

The condition worsened to the point of trips to the bathroom at night every fifteen minutes. In desperation and feeling constantly terrible, I went to a wholistic medical doctor who tried to help with no avail. He suspected I had what he called "Big C." I have reason to believe he may have been a charading charlatan disguised as a successful doctor. He sent me to Mexico for supposedly natural treatments which included one shot a day, some pills, a special diet and daily enemas for six weeks. Finally, their exames indicated the so called "cancer" was gone and I went home.

The following months unfolded with more swelling and the same loss of sleep after paying thousands of dollars for the treatments below the border.

Back to another urologist I went when I discovered my problem wasn't cancer, but infection I thought, so I resumed antibiotics which knocked out the infection and also made me realize after a lot of study, cancer and infection had similarities where both were cell deterioration and tended to "feed" on each other.

Although I had been generally quite wholistic conducting my health affairs in a natural manner as possible without drugs or surgery beside antibiotics, I did draw as many strings together from the medical aspect (mostly examinations) and the natural manner over a long period of time testing many supplemental remedies, hygienic mannerisms, diets, psychological formulation, attitude, beliefs and new and profound self-programming. It eventually began strengthening normal cells while slowly reducing the swelling and cancer cell tendency.

More time passed and I began to ease off on my seemingly well disciplined rules because I thought I had gained immunity to acquiring cancer.

Low and behold, was I in for a surprise from relaxing too much. My doctor's office called and said to go to the urologist and get checked. My PSA reading for cancer of the prostate was up to 12 which was reason for alarm. The urologist extracted biopsies, found cancerous cells and issued my "rights" of treatments.

Once again, together with my primary medical doctor, I made the decision to decline any treatment except my own. My doctor didn't accept any responsibility in relationship with my decision. He remained indifferent.

Months passed and I had a PSA check to discover, using my own natural methods of slowing the cell infested disease, it had dropped from 12 to 7. Many more months unveiled a count 7 to 5 and still moving down. The cancer was diminishing.

After those very good figures, I was convinced the process was moving in the right direction. I have continued to innovate with this progress while the numbers are moving down.

During those discovery years, I also had two skin cancer growths removed from the surface of my nose. Around the time just prior to hearing of my PSA dropping, I noticed another cancer growth beginning to form on my nose. I left it alone and as the months rolled by, I diligently exercised my old and newly acquired methods of reducing the carcinogenic, genetic and toxic influences toward cancer formation subsequently reducing and dissolving the newly appearing growth and none have returned since.

This experience of allowing nature to maintain a cancer free body is similar to the way people obviously lived without cancer in the very old centuries of time with pure water, pure air, pure food, purity in barter exchanges, purity in genetical descendancy and many other purities that prevented cancer misery. Now, almost everything we touch is contaminated. No wonder cancer has tended to prevail so strongly.

I have evaluated one aspect of cancer growth as being a cell attraction to almost any adverse substance or condition. The cancer experiences I encountered with my prostate and nose has fairly strong evidence of these adverse substances being an appetite for the growths. Here is why:

I lived with nonthreatening "and" life threatening infections most of my younger life. When I was a teenager, I had one mountainous pus pimple infection after another called boils many times with a life threatening red line moving toward my vital points which meant certain death once it arrived at the heart or brain. In those days, it was a game I played to see how big the mountains of pus would get before I popped them out with a coke bottle of heated water that created a vacuum. They healed up, but kept returning. It was, indeed, a form of blood poisoning. I had little knowledge of cause and effect theory then and only instinctly guessed it was because of the type of food I was consuming. I had "no" knowledge of an immune system gone amok due to genetic and several factors mentioned in this book.

After gaining knowledge where my health problems could be very serious, I began my health conscious practices as a very young teenager eliminating junk food and eating carrots etc. and instinctively, reducing sweets, then ice cream and deep fried food. That stopped the boils. What was left were teenage pimples that continued for many years. I nursed them along popping and cleaning them. Finally well into my twenties, I went to an allergist and discovered I had a long list of food allergies. I was given shots to counteract the affects which deceived me to believe I was cured. How mistaken I was. I quit the shots.

I worked hard and played hard. I always had to be the best, but in the process, I was always worn out and didn't know why. The years flew by and I slowly became a health fanatic through study and efforts practiced. I lived with infection all those years and outgrew and offset a lot of it, but the underlying persistence stayed with me through discipline along with cheating on my diet once in a while until I was finally faced with even a more strict diet.

The effects of age, diet complications, genetics tendencies etc. at around 35 began to creep in and by 40, my prostate swelling continued and matured with infection.

My further pursuance in health and psychology brought eventual wholistic relief of skin cancer and prostate cancer mostly with natural methods.

Isn't it amazing and ironic how prolonged infection can turn to cancer. It's enough to make this author/victim to believe there is a connection in contrast to some medical views.

Every time I released my discipline with diet and other contributing factors to infection, the infection returned.

Every time I released my discipline of diet and other contributing factors with cancer, it mutated.

The more I choose to believe, preach, program and practice my wholistic methods for offsetting self-inflicted disease, the more and better results I receive. The cancer mutation on my nose has stopped and my prostate has diminished constantly in the direction toward zero with natural methods.

I am reasonably convinced if everyone would believe, support and faithfully practice wholistic and philosophical methods while one enhances with the other, results will thrive in a healthier and more cooperatively stable community of mankind. I am also aware of exceptional cases needing surgery which may be termed as radical or immediate attention as an emergency.

The mental affects the physical and the physical affects the mental. My body knows how, after lots of disciplinary programming and practicing wholistic ways, it cannot get away with performing an attack of self-inflicted illness symptoms.

The master key toward preventing and stopping cancer growth is to develop a system of patience along with the necessary skills and continue them relentlessly as a way of life since we all have or acquire some form of vulnerability to human flaws.

Many allergies have contributed toward cell deterioration and interpreted as cancer. Get checked periodically even when you are confidently into preventive methods and have proven they work.

Continuous irritated, festered or infected areas of the human system may perform in their relentless manner due to genetically inherited traits that can be reduced in intensity with the use of specific herbs, supplements and other natural methods well known in the field of wholistic health such as chiropractic, acupuncture, emotional therapy and possibly some homeopathic treatment guided by a professional along with all the previously mentioned suggestions.

Most people have some type of allergy. We are born with them and can only attempt to offset the symptoms until Earth becomes pure again.

Care and caution must be exercised in the use of "any" orally consumed substances to avoid toxic affects from overdosing. Professional guidance is usually better.

While allergic tendencies are reduced, cancer tendencies have been known to reduce at the same time. The natural body works natural wonders with natural remedies.

When one asks how long it will take to turn cancer infestation around or reverse it, one must understand it doesn't really turn around or go backward. It just stops what it had been doing. Cancer growth is the same as life. What keeps people alive? Food and liquid. Don't feed them and they die. Cancer is the same. Feed them with the cancer factors mentioned and they will stay alive. Withdraw them and they will become inactive.

When one feels bad with cancer, that is a whole body indication of highly influenced sick tendencies on all the body's cells. There are more specific areas, glands or organs etc. breaking down from any or all the influential factors mentioned in this book periodically. That or those areas usually break down initially, become cancerous, then mutate further in their process. Remember, feeling bad throughout doesn't mean cancer will occur throughout the body. Most of the time, feeling bad or tired all the time means the mind and body's cells are or have been out of tune or collectively low on their sources of normal energy. Not feeling well is usually "all over." One might call it a warning or an indication the whole system has been weakening maybe for a long time; possibly many years. I have experienced it and needed strengthening so the cells could maintain a healthier strength. Where cancer is concerned, that means "resistance" strength, not muscle strength. A strong and resisting immune system contributing toward preventing cancer growth or the support of it can increase its resistance to the disease.

Everyone has some kind of weakness. Breasts for women and prostate glands for men are classic weaknesses or vulnerabilities. Note: The two most susceptible organs of breast and prostate gland require a healthy hormonal balance. When that balance is off the wayside, the candidacy for cancer increases. One might say that candidacy for cancer applies when one doesn't maintain a healthy immune system. Get checked and correct it.

Once again, how long does it take to reduce cancer growth? Generally, if it took a long time to form, it may take a similar length of time to stop it completely depending on the belief, approach and disciplined methods applied. However, don't dwindle on it with any noncreative incentives. Whatever the length of time, it's far better to reduce it down knowing it won't consume the whole body system. Shrinking it is great!

After all has been said about preventing, managing and ending cancer in these scripts, some last words I have for you is to remember; cancer doesn't really have to be killed, shattered, eradicated or destroyed etc. for it to stop its affect on the body. It will cease its persistence when it can no longer "feed" on strength boosted cells. When the mind finally is convinced it has control over the overall situation of strengthening the immune system, it will have the confidence to continue in that wonderfully acquired and equipped ability to control the self. Furthermore, when the body becomes thoroughly convinced through its communicating brain of neurons and transmitters, it either accepts the informed demands of the brain's headquarters (the individual's mind) and acts accordingly by changing body function or it hesitates for a length of time in its response or even further can reject the individual's demand due to insufficient programming and/or belief.

If that insufficient programming appears to be the case, a little more sincere effort in acquiring sufficient belief and usable knowledge may be necessary to bolster the driving force in the brain. It's all a matter of accepting the power of being responsible. Oh, what a great power that is!

Do not ever consider there being anything "really" fair in this life. Stop a bit and realize that helps to understand why some of us don't suffer with health problems or much less anyway—and some of us have to work harder maintaining it constantly. Let us not waste energy fretting over it and get to our beckoning call of reducing cancer. We can't be bothered by it. We have too many things to do in this life. We "are" how we program ourselves.

I, your author, write about cause, purpose, effect and meaning. That's my purpose, certainly not for a purpose of preparing myself for a career in the field of health or psychology with a prestigious title before or after my name. I'm just me.

The preceding chapters on cancer were more of a generalization of the subject. This book hasn't been presented as a textbook on the subject. This book has been offered more as a controversial or disputatious nature with attempts to help arrive at bottom line benefits for eliminating cancer possibly along with several other self-inflicted diseases.

I have helped others reduce their cancer mutation to the remission state and thoroughly believe in natural methods all the more observing their progress as well as mine. Some continue with their good progress by adopting and living with this lifestyle. Others, unfortunately by their lack of steady adaptation, resumed their old free wheeling habits that stimulated cancer and followed their inevitable destiny. They surrendered. They allowed defeat. Who knows, maybe their genetic tendencies, rearing days, social and chemical etc., influences overwhelmed them into submission to the forces. Some people commit suicide because of such forces. Things got out of hand!

I emphasize gaining constant understanding of what supports determination in overcoming self-inflicted disease as compared to either relinquishing an opportunity to whip a disease or submitting to what may "seem" as an overwhelming and dominate mental load too strong to resist. Yes, the question that may elevate one above that mental load is, "What permits that thinking" and find a creative answer.

If anyone suffers from those seemingly mental loads, be sure to probe into getting or forming some answers to, "What permits that thinking" and remember, success achieved breads on success gained. Rising above our weak and previously programmed tendencies are richly rewarding.

After we study and become more aware of cancer function, its affects, its options in approach of preventing or eliminating it, wholistic (natural) methods work better not allowing room in the mind of how bad the condition can get when one is seriously handling the challenge of control "over" it. Dwelling on how bad it can get only has a potential of stimulating its tendency to mutate. There is also a strong tendency for many people, while thinking and/or talking about how bad it can get, to utilize that consciousness as mind programming toward the promotion of cancer mutation. Watch it! Don't be a victim of your own thinking. That can become a detrimental belief.

First in line in conquering this disease is to gather the contributing factors to cancer (the study). Second, sort them out as perspectively as possible. Third, establish a dependable belief and fourth, relentlessly practice an optimistic plan that gains more confidence in maybe slow, but noticeably good results that perpetuates more of the same. This is well worth looking forward to in preventing or managing cancer. Stay focused on the methods, the belief and the relentless approach in the planned efforts. Keep it going. It's available and waiting. I chose to do it and it works well. You can too.

Repeating this study along with its practice is "very" helpful in the success of this challenge. It'll be like giving the efforts put forth an extra "boost."

Preventing cancer is basically the same as eliminating it. It really works while never forgetting conventionally established methods may be better for those who are convinced they are. They both have their advantages.

The whole issue of dealing with preventing or eliminating cancer is surrounded by alternatives of which a person, a family, an association or a whole society of people can largely benefit from beside the possible benefits they currently have.

Health successes aren't necessarily all derived from college educated professionals. Give them a break. You and I can be a significant part of that life journey of experiences by reducing the complexities of it all in the following manner more or less depending on the intellectual, mental or emotional state of mind a person is made up of at the time and their willingness to participate as follows:

#1. If relaxing is a problem, learn to relax first. It can be of great help in getting in touch with what one desires and sticking with it. Natural methods are great. Be patient and perseverant.

#2. Study the self by noticing how the self reacts to everything done every day. Make vocal suggestions of what changes and improvements one is willing to make within every day and continue that programming.

#3. Study and ask questions to whoever about nutrition, toxin exposure, body and mind development and gaining confidence in the self.

#4. Watch health programs on TV. Attend health seminars.

#5. Finish this list by adopting creative ideas for health often and make corrections on them. That's what I do and what I will continue to do for better health and longer life. That's good growth.

Whatever your choices may be in approach and procedure, make it patiently persistent and relentless. That's where and when the best results unfold. Cancer "is" preventable and conquerable. We just need to get serious in focusing in on it and managing it to win and stay won. If you like what you have studied here, see my list of books in back for your reading purposes. There are many unfolding as time passes.

A couple of last, but not least, clues for getting control over the cancer problem which is about the basis of preventing cancer, leading ourselves through it and/or bringing it to a stop. This is simply living with, maintaining and/or building a strong immune system. Some have it and some do not; maybe because of never really understanding what its function is.

The immune system exists throughout the body as a source of energy which fights off virus protein and cancer cells. When its strength is normal, it rids the body's system of the adverse attacking and recuperates the body back to normal. When its weak, the body is unable to resist the attackers and the disease grows until the limp immune system wears down the virus, but probably not the cancer cells without intelligently assisted health improvement determination.

A weak immune system needs strengthening to ward off adverse health with the use of a balanced diet with what amounts to an established health ratio of a majority of alkaline food (vegetables and fruit) and a minority of acid food (meat, dairy, nuts, grains, alcohol and the list is long. This is referred to as a PH balance of alkaline/acid food which is essential in resisting cancer development. Practice it well. It can also shed pounds off the body. These foods are listed in my book "Staying Alive On Planet Earth" #1. See the list.

Some medical and chiropractic doctors are nutritionally professed with diet, supplementation and immune system guidance. This is advised for those who are insufficiently prepared for handling the commitments this book displays. Professional guidance is always recommended especially when one is maintaining a very strict diet.

Check with professional nutritionists or health food stores for the following which is known for combating and/or preventing cancer when the right amount is determined and consumed:

glutathione	bromelain	mistletoe	minerals	beta-carotene
chaparral	echinacea	Elderberry	Gensing	Grapeseed extract
astragalus	antioxidants	saffron	vitamin c&d	sodium potassium

Advanced cancer has a strong tendency to take over control of the body when one hasn't had regular physical examinations; especially when noticeable changes occur in the body. Don't put it off! Don't let cancer sneak up on you. Don't feed cancer the junk and elements it craves. "Do" feed the body and mind the natural philosophy and nutrients the body and mind thrives on for staying strong and resisting such annoying and potentially deadly sources of infiltration as cancer does.

Don't forget to reduce stress whenever you can. It "does" contribute toward the development of cancer in many people and creeps in several different ways. Search for material on it.

Just as a reminder, the mind was given to us, especially in this time of rushing around, for being responsible for preventing and/or managing self-inflicted disease. Let us practice that responsibility for preventing or reducing cancer development "before" it becomes unmanageable.

If you decide to adapt with the natural methods of better health maintenance and preventing or controlling cancer, be unbendingly patient while continuing your acquired methods and challenge of gaining more knowledge on this subject. It pays. L.E.M.

Your author, Lloyd E. McIlveen unveils a chronological list of many and various book subjects presenting controversial, educational, uplifting, futuristic, self-helping, philosophical, psychological, entertaining and other stimulating concepts of which are and will be displayed with brief descriptions of each book as follows:

1. "Evaluating Outdated Beliefs" This is a report, viewed through the perception of your author of the evolutionary process and changes occurring in belief; especially in the area of religion and spirituality, This was designed for the benefit of broadening individual perception, perspective and viewing "another" plane of belief while revealing fallacies in theological indoctrination. This is an improved revision of the book's origin.

2. "Staying Alive On Planet Earth I" This is a psychology of health required to stabilize and maintain better health for the benefit of living

a much longer life. Source: A lifetime of study, problems, recoveries and many successes more in natural methods.

3. "Understanding Loss To Relieve The Anguish" Loss of anything involves many distractions and disrupting emotional disarray. Gaining greater understanding of these emotions offsets the misery of them and enhances optimism of confidence and support for emotional weakness before, at and during the time of loss.

4. "Understanding Preventing And Eliminating Cancer" presents new views on the wonders of natural methods for practical use.

5. "Paradox Of Progress Unfolding I" This is a tale told by a man "many" centuries into the future about an exciting, overwhelming and terrifying occurrence on planet Earth as a result of their wondrous progress around the time of 2300 A.D. Hang onto your seats! #2 is a second issue later on the list.

6. "Offsetting Climate Change And Nuclear Waste Contamination" This view of the two exposes the hazards, inevitabilities and possible solutions needed now for preventing a "too late" disaster that will affect all living beings too soon.

7. "What God Is And Is Not" This is a study of spiritual possibilities designed, not particularly to remold conventional mannerisms of belief, but to open and expand perception in the most controversial subject of mankind; the subject of God and whether mankind will or won't expand that consciousness along with all progress and growth on Earth and in the universe.

8. "Kids Of The Crick" This is a story of four old fashioned country kids setting out on a weekend adventure in their countryside of tall grass, mountains, rivers, animals, caves and strange living beings. Sometimes, they aren't sure whether it's all real or not.

9. "Paradox Of Destiny Explained" eliminates the mysteries, facades, fantasies and deceptions of how, where, way and when we do what we do and opens new possibilities for expanding our beliefs and consciousness pertaining to this study of available options that may influence insight for growth, change or even justify present mannerisms of what may control the individual, planet Earth or the whole universe and is not zealous, fanatic or bigoted; only assertively revealing.

10. "Paradox Of Progress Unfolding 2" This book is a continued fiction story and can be considered exemplary of "major" human changes that alienated millions of people to another planet in the future. They are led by the elements of unexpected surprises of which is par for the course with gutsy space pioneers. The first "Paradox Of Progress Unfolding I" must be read first to understand and appreciate the disproportional attitudes

and positions of people on a threshold of major change and disasters upon them. This is not only a tale of travel, trials and tribulations, it is philosophically stimulating and adds toward future insightful expansion of the human species.

11. "Staying Alive On Planet Earth 2" This is an extended version of the original psychology of health for living a longer life. More knowledge allows more life.

12. "Preventing The Doom Of Mankind" This is a stimulating, vitalizing and somewhat shocking description of how mankind is "truly" faced with extinction in the "near" future due to their own faults of progress. It's very educational and needed now to help offset that inevitability where the odds dictate we will all perish if we don't adhere to this offsetting of which "is" possible to achieve.

13. "Spiritual Transformation Of The Fourth Millennium" Old-time conventional religion

is fading. New-time spirituality is on the rise. Objective realism is the prime issue here for future inclined thinking and believing.

14. "Understanding The Science Of Creative Mind" This is a study for discovering, developing and practicing a psychological powerhouse within for conquering the unconquerable, achieving the impossible or doing things no one has done all depending on, of course, the makeup and determination of the individual. This study brings out a greater potential of the individual's abilities when taken seriously. This was compiled from a lifetime of study and experience from your author.

15. "Living to 150" is a guidance program for intentions of anyone desiring a longer than longer life which is insightfully and innovatively educational for that purpose.

16. "The Act Of Getting One's Act Together" If anyone, business or nation wants to develop

their stance, priorities and position in life, this is a chance for them to get their act together more than ever.

17. "Making Changes From This Point Forward" The design of this book is for the purpose of preventing repeated mistakes of unforeseen surprises due to what we weren't or aren't aware of that did, can or will happen again. It's all about gaining or rearranging change consciousness in this area.

18. "Relationships For All" This is a carefully arranged view of how relationships can function much better when initiated or guided by the experiences of many experts and your author who have had failures and successes in their very human encounters. The experiences of more relationships result in wiser judgments and approaches to others.

19. "The We Between Us" helps us in discovering who is good for us and who is not. First it is a study in the book. Then it is a study with

people of what exists in two party's minds (individuals business or nations) when first confronted. A real time saver in evaluating possible compatibility or not between the two for anyone. It works.

20. "Passion Of Dance" This is a narrative on progress, value and guidance for the dance inclined. It's informative and inspiring with its history and recent magnetism.

21. "Open That Door" to love. This book is comprehensively all about love. It's not a storybook. It clears up the differences of love that causes misunderstanding, suspicion and deception.

22. "Get The Spirit" This book describes controversial and somewhat intertwined conventional views of spirit, spirits and spirituality. This book untangles the "usual" views and presents a more perspective manner of living with these concepts of mind.

23. "Stories Of What They Couldn't Or Wouldn't Tell" Ages are from babies to 100 years; twenty four of them.

24. "Improving On Love And Relationships" This one is two books in one. Part one "Open That Door" is a psychology of love that enhances perspective to understand and adapt to a very popular, but deceiving, repressed and ignored emotion; love. Part two covers "Relationships For All" which elaborates on origination, different types, significance, deceptions, desires, experiences, communication, possibilities, future and guidance of relationships. It's comprehensive and also derived from a lifetime of relationship experiences and serious study.

Index